AN ADVERSARY IN HEAVEN

HARVARD SEMITIC MUSEUM

HARVARD SEMITIC MONOGRAPHS

edited by
Frank Moore Cross

Number 43
AN ADVERSARY IN HEAVEN
śāṭān in the Hebrew Bible

by
Peggy L. Day

Peggy L. Day

AN ADVERSARY IN HEAVEN
$\underline{ś}\bar{a}\d{t}\bar{a}\underline{n}$ in the Hebrew Bible

Scholars Press
Atlanta, Georgia

AN ADVERSARY IN HEAVEN

śāṭān in the Hebrew Bible

by
Peggy L. Day

Library of Congress Cataloging in Publication Data

Day, Peggy Lynne.
An Adversary in Heaven : Satan in the Hebrew Bible / Peggy L. Day.
p. cm. -- (Harvard Semitic monographs ; no. 43)
Bibliography: p.
ISBN 1-55540-248-8(alk. paper)
1. Devil--Biblical teaching. 2. Satan (The Hebrew word)
3. Bible. O.T.--Criticism, interpretation, etc. I. Title.
II. Series.
BS1199.D4D39 1988 88-19170
235'.47--dc19

Printed in the United States of America
on acid-free paper

In loving memory of my parents,

Robert David and Renée Caroline Day

CONTENTS

Preface

This monograph is a revised version of my 1986 Harvard doctoral dissertation, "*śāṭān* in the Hebrew Bible." I had been warned repeatedly by those more experienced than I in the book-writing process that a project is never really finished: at some point, one simply must make the decision to stop working on it. I now realize how true this is.

I gladly join the chorus of voices who have sung the praises of Frank Moore Cross, and acknowledge that without his inspiration and guidance this would have been a very different piece of work. Reading *Ludlul bēl nēmeqi* with William Moran greatly enriched my understanding of the *śāṭān* in Job, and the opportunity to discuss deuterocanonical literature and Qumran with John Strugnell enabled me to shape my Chronicles chapter. Michael Coogan provided not only a valuable critique of the entire dissertation but also a sympathetic ear, and the influence of Paul Hanson's work on the restoration period is readily evident in my discussion of Zechariah 3. Without Thomas Lambdin's guidance I could not have written the chapter on etymology. Gerald Janzen provided a challenging counterpoint to my ideas about Job, and James Kugel kept us all honest. Doug Gropp gave generously of his time to proofread and copy-edit the manuscript at the dissertation stage.

Revision of the dissertation was undertaken in the Religious Studies Reading Room at my alma mater, the University of British Columbia. I would like to thank Paul Mosca for making it possible for me to work there. More importantly, I thank him for his continued encouragement and friendship, and for providing me with a model of what it means to be a good teacher. To my undergraduate advisor Hanna Kassis I owe a special debt both for awakening me to the world of Near Eastern studies and for suggesting that I do doctoral work at a place called Harvard. I had certainly heard of the place but had no idea where it was, although I suspected that it was in England.

To my Makioka sisters Carol McGauley and Cathleen Smith, and to Jaime Smith and Hansi and David Durlach, thank you for being part of my extended and eclectic family. Without your emotional support the purgatory of graduate work would have been pure hell.

As the daughter of parents who had grade eight educations, my doing a doctorate at Harvard was not a natural turn of events either for me or for them. To their everlasting credit they supported me in something that they really didn't understand. Had I become an arc welder, they would have reacted in the same way. For the freedom that they gave me to be me, this volume is dedicated to them.

Peggy L. Day
Trinity College, Toronto
June 10, 1988

Abbreviations

The abbreviations used in this work follow those listed in the _Catholic Biblical Quarterly_ 38 (1976) 438-453.

Chapter 1

INTRODUCTION

This study focuses on the four passages in the Hebrew Bible (Num 22:22-35; Zech 3:1-7; Job 1-2; 1 Chr 21:1-22:1) in which the noun *śāṭān* is used to describe a heavenly being. Its most fundamental debt is to that stream of modern scholarship which, since the finds at Ugarit in the 1930s, has recognized that the ancient Near Eastern concept of a divine council, and the function of that council as a judiciary body, is very much alive in the biblical texts. Building on the insights of scholars such as H. Wheeler Robinson,[1] G. Ernest Wright,[2] and Frank Moore Cross,[3] it has become increasingly clear that Yahweh, like the Canaanite god El, was envisaged as presiding over a council of heavenly beings. Among the primary functions of this divine assembly was the dispensation of justice,[4] both within

----

1. "The Council of Yahweh," *JTS* 45 (1944) 151-157.

2. *The Old Testament Against its Enviroment* (Chicago: Henry Regnery, 1950) 30-41.

3. "The Council of Yahweh in Second Isaiah," *JNES* 12 (1953) 274-277. See also the literature cited by Cross in this article.

4. Note, for example, the burgeoning literature on the prophetic *rîb*. A comprehensive bibliography can be found in Michael de Roche's recent article ("Yahweh's *Rîb* Against Israel: A Re-Assessment of the So-Called 'Prophetic Lawsuit' in the Preexilic Prophets," *JBL* 102 [1983] 563-574, esp. 563-564). De Roche's own position is that "lawsuit" is a misnomer because, in order for a dispute to be strictly judicial, the adjudicating body must be distinct from the litigants, and empowered to

the celestial realm itself (Ps 82) and in relation to the terrestrial sphere (1 Kgs 22:19-22).[5] Recognition of this forensic function of the divine assembly brings the council scenes envisaged in the prologue to Job and in Zechariah 3 into sharper focus. Extrapolating from this, and noting that 1 Chr 21:1 employs a technical term typical of participation in the divine council, it is possible that *śāṭān* in 1 Chr 21:1 should also be understood forensically.

----

hand down a binding decision (p. 565). The prophetic *rîb* does not qualify as a lawsuit because Yahweh, involved as a litigant, does not appeal to an independent third party to resolve disputes (p. 570). De Roche draws upon Simon Roberts (*Order and Dispute: An Introduction to Legal Anthropology* [Harmondsworth: Penguin, 1979] 17-29) for his discussion of the various modes of conflict resolution. Roberts himself notes (*Order and Dispute*, 71) that categories of conflict resolution tend to blend into one another, and this observation is seconded by Paul Bohannan ("The Differing Realms of Law," P. Bohannan [ed.], *Law and Warfare* [New York: Natural History Press, 1967] 44), who prefers to speak of "zones of transition" between that which is unquestionably legal and that which is not. Furthermore, Roberts cautions (*Order and Dispute*, 18) that we must pay attention to how a given society defines its interrelationships. We know that the agreement between Yahweh and Israel was described in terms of a covenant relationship, a legal contract that carried with it certain stipulations. We should expect, therefore, that when those stipulations were transgressed, the ensuing complaint (*rîb*) was understood as a legal action. Perhaps "lawsuit" is not the most appropriate term to describe this action, but to deny the *rîb* legal status is, I think, to stretch the point beyond its usefulness. This point aside, de Roche has performed a valuable service by introducing comparative anthropological theory into the discussion of the biblical legal process.

5. Cf. James Ackerman, "An Exegetical Study of Psalm 82," Th.D. dissertation, Harvard University, 1966, esp. 178-272; E. Theodore Mullen, *The Assembly of the Gods: The Divine Council in Canaanite and Early Hebrew Literature* (HSM 24; Chico: Scholars, 1980) 226-244.

Aside from the present study, the only in-depth, book-length examination of the four passages which feature a celestial *śāṭān* was published by Rivkah Kluger in 1948.[6] Since that time a few short dictionary articles have appeared,[7] but their focus has been Satan and not *śāṭān*, hence the Hebrew Bible texts have been treated summarily. Herbert Haag's *Teufelsglaube* appeared in 1974. It devotes approximately twenty pages to Satan in the Old Testament, and does not treat Numbers 22. In short, with the exception of brief notes in biblical commentaries, very little has been written on *śāṭān* since 1948.

Since 1948, there have been some radical shifts in both approaches toward and conclusions reached about all four of the contexts in which a heavenly *śāṭān* appears. Our understanding of the Balaam cycle (Num 22-24) has been enriched by the finds made at Deir ᶜAllā, which provide an extra-biblical vantage point from which to view the biblical Balaam traditions. The story of Balaam and the ass (Num 22:22-35) in which Yahweh's messenger is dispatched *lĕśāṭān* had, until recently, been attributed to epic (J) tradition, and thus the passage was viewed as by far the earliest reference to a celestial *śāṭān*. This source attribution has been recently and repeatedly challenged, and although no specific consensus has been reached, the ass story

----

6. "Die Gestalt des Satans im Alten Testament," C. G. Jung (ed.), *Symbolik des Geistes* (Zurich: Rascher, 1948). This was translated into English and republished in 1967 as *Satan in the Old Testament*, but was not updated comprehensively.

7. Most notably, T. H. Gaster, "Satan," *IDB* vol. 4, 224-228 (1962). G. von Rad's "*diabolos*" (*TDNT* vol. 2, 72-81) was published in 1964 but is an unrevised translation of a 1935 *TWNT* article.

increasingly is being viewed as a product of the sixth century B.C.E. or later.[8]

Job scholarship also has been changing. Whereas earlier studies tended to view the book atomistically and claim that the various sections of the book (i.e. prologue, dialogues, whirlwind speeches, etc.) were ill-fitted together, more recent treatments, such as the commentaries of Norman Habel (1985) and J. Gerald Janzen (1985), have identified signals of continuity amongst and between the book's major parts. The importance of the role that irony plays in the book of Job also is being recognized, and these two sensitivities taken together make it plausible to see resonances of the prologue's śāṭān in the other sections of the book.

Due primarily to Christian Jeremias' detailed study of the visions of Zechariah (1977) and Paul Hanson's sociologically oriented investigation of power struggles and politics in the restoration community (1979), the issues underlying Zechariah 3 have been brought into clearer focus. In Zechariah 3 Joshua the high priest can no longer be viewed as functioning as a symbol of the entire (i.e. united) community. Rather, the vision functions to legitimate Joshua in the face of opposition originating from within the restoration community itself. Our understanding of the role of the śāṭān in this passage must be adjusted accordingly.

Research into the date and purpose of the books of Chronicles also has taken recently a radical turn. Prior to the 1960s, Chronicles-Ezra-Nehemiah was viewed

----

8. Cf. the discussion and footnotes in chapter 4.

as basically a single composition. David Noel Freedman (1961), Sara Japhet (1968), and Frank Moore Cross (1975) have been instrumental in disentangling the Chronicler's work from the books of Ezra-Nehemiah, and have proposed both a thematic and chronological disjuncture between Chronicles and Ezra-Nehemiah. Insight into the way that the Chronicler treated his sources has been provided by 4QSam[a] and has been examined in detail by Steven McKenzie (1985). In short, the combined fruits of recent research make it less likely, in my opinion, that *śāṭān* in 1 Chronicles 21 is a proper name.

In addition to benefitting from the streams of scholarship described briefly above, this study differs from previous studies in that it sees no Satan in the Hebrew Bible. Either explicitly[9] or implicitly,[10] the vast bulk of work on the noun *śāṭān* as it is used in the celestial sphere has been developmentally oriented. By this I mean that the end product - Satan - is always in sight, as if latent in the noun itself was some kind of knowledge of where it was headed. The "character" or "personality" of *śāṭān* (or rather, the Satan) is typically discussed, and questions posed as to the order in which he acquired his various nefarious qualities, and the process by which he became estranged from God. Whereas these may be valid questions when asked from an historically later perspective, they are not valid in the context of the Hebrew Bible if the Hebrew Bible knows no Satan. The developmental approach culminates in the work

----

9. See the review of scholarship presented below.

10. For example, scholars typically refer to "the Satan" in Job, "the Satan" in Zechariah, etc.. Even though the definite article is retained, capitalization of the noun implies that Satan nevertheless lurks somewhere in gestation, awaiting full birth.

of Rivkah Schärf Kluger,[11] whose thesis is that, by studying the texts that mention a celestial ś̱ā̱ṭā̱ṉ, we are able to witness a development within "the divine personality,"[12] the progressive (and successful) cleansing of God's dark side,[13] a goal finally achieved in 1 Chronicles 21 where ś̱ā̱ṭā̱ṉ is the independent personality Satan. As we shall see in the chapter dealing with 1 Chr 21:1-22:1, there is absolutely no evidence to indicate that ś̱ā̱ṭā̱ṉ in this passage should be translated as a proper name. Rather, ś̱ā̱ṭā̱ṉ in 1 Chr 21:1 refers to an unnamed member of the celestial assembly. Furthermore, this ś̱ā̱ṭā̱ṉ need not necessarily be identified with the heavenly being who raises objections concerning Joshua's suitability for the high priesthood (Zech 3:1-7), nor with the ś̱ā̱ṭā̱ṉ who questions Job's motives for worshipping Yahweh (Job 1-2).

Many of the scholars who have remarked upon the noun ś̱ā̱ṭā̱ṉ as it is used in the heavenly sphere have done so within the context of commentaries dealing with one or more of the specific passages, and consequently I shall enter into dialogue with their opinions when discussing the appropriate passages. There have, however, been a few independent studies, either dealing with the origins of Satan in particular or as a part of works dealing with evil, demons, and devils, and it is to these that I shall briefly turn.

----

11. "Die Gestalt des Satans im Alten Testament," Carl G. Jung (ed.), Symbolik des Geistes (Zurich: Rascher, 1948). Republished as Satan in the Old Testament (Evanston: Northwestern, 1967). All references will be to the 1967 English edition.

12. Kluger, Satan, 79, 87.

13. Kluger, Satan, 159.

The scholar commonly credited with writing the first modern history of the devil is Gustav Roskoff.[14] In the roughly seven pages devoted to Satan in the Old Testament, Roskoff sewed the first seeds of the developmental approach. Roskoff took as his earliest text the book of Job in which, he reasoned, Satan could not have been an enemy of God's will because he appears among the angels.[15] In Job, Satan is a tool to prove human purity; in earlier Hebrew belief, Yahweh did the testing (Gen 22).[16] In Zechariah there is a development in the character of Satan because he becomes an accuser, and is the opponent of humankind. (For Roskoff, Joshua represents Israel.)[17] As is evident, Roskoff's treatment of the *śāṭān* in Job was not informed by recognition that the scene is set in the heavenly tribunal, and therefore the fact that the *śāṭān* of Zechariah 3 acts as an accuser cannot be viewed as a development. Furthermore, as I shall demonstrate in the chapter dealing with Zech 3:1-7, Joshua represents neither humanity in general nor all Israel, and thus the *śāṭān* of Zechariah 3 is not the opponent of humankind.

Karl Marti's "Zwei Studien zu Sacharja: 1. Der Ursprung des Satans"[18] was one of the first in a series

----

14. *Geschichte des Teufels* (Leipzig: Brockhaus, 1869). Note, however, the article by Diestel ("Set=Typhon, Asahel und Satan," *ZHT* 30 [1860] 159-217).

15. Roskoff, *Geschichte*, 187.

16. Roskoff, *Geschichte*, 188.

17. Roskoff, *Geschichte*, 189.

18. *TSK* 65 (1892) 207-245.

of modern attempts to identify the origin of Satan.[19] Marti offered a psychological explanation,[20] postulating that Zechariah's *śāṭān* figure is the personified doubt of Zechariah's community, a doubt that questions God's grace.[21] For Marti, Zechariah created the Satan[22] just as he had created, for instance, the woman in the ephah. The Satan opposes pardoning the people (again, Joshua is understood to represent the community) because they remain guilty of contravening Yahweh's will.[23] As we shall see, Zech 3:1-7 does not share the primary characteristics of the other seven visions in Zechariah 1-8, and therefore it is incorrect to argue that, as Zechariah created the woman in the ephah, so he created the *śāṭān*. Unlike Roskoff, Marti saw the *śāṭān* of Job as a development beyond the *śāṭān* of Zechariah because in Job, the *śāṭān* is at home in heaven, and because the Joban *śāṭān* is evil.[24] 1 Chr 21:1 is yet a further development because Satan relishes persecuting humankind.[25]

----

19. Prior to Marti, B. Stade (*Geschichte des Volkes Israel* [Berlin: G. Grote, 1888] 243), for instance, had made in passing the remark that Satan was a pre-Yahwistic demon who, with the development of angels, was taken over into that category.

20. "Zwei Studien," 236. Marti was writing at the time when Freud was beginning to publish his early studies.

21. "Zwei Studien," 235.

22. "Zwei Studien," 235, 242.

23. "Zwei Studien," 216, 231, 242.

24. "Zwei Studien," 243.

25. "Zwei Studien," 244.

With Hans Duhm[26] we return to the thesis that Job, not Zechariah, is the most primitive context to mention the Satan. Duhm used the Joban portrayal to arrive at the original character of Satan, which he understood to be the merciless enemy, the personification of the malice of fate.[27] For Duhm, Zechariah 3 demonstrated that the people's idea of Satan had changed in what he called the post-exilic theological system; Satan could no longer talk freely with Yahweh as he did in Job.[28] By the time of Zechariah, Satan's role had become particularized to parallel the office of king's accuser.[29] 1 Chr 21:1 demonstrated a further development toward the New Testament Satan because in Chronicles, Satan is a seducer, not an accuser.[30] Duhm's point about the office of king's accuser will be dealt with in the section treating the meaning of *śāṭān*. For the moment, note simply that Duhm did not recognize the forensic dimensions of Job 1-2, and that he understood *śāṭān* in 1 Chronicles 21 to be a proper name.

In addition to being developmentally oriented, the studies reviewed above are similar in that they confined their respective discussions of *śāṭān* basically to three texts (Job 1-2; Zech 3; 1 Chr 21) and derived the "primitive" character or meaning of *śāṭān* (and, by extension, Satan) from either Job or Zechariah, depending on which of these two was deemed earlier. There was no

----

26. *Die bösen Geister im Alten Testament* (Tübingen: J.C.B. Mohr, 1904).

27. *Die bösen Geister*, 19.

28. *Die bösen Geister*, 59.

29. *Die bösen Geister*, 60.

30. *Die bösen Geister*, 61.

serious attempt to bring Num 22:22-35 into the discussion, nor to examine the contexts in which *śāṭān* refers to a non-celestial figure.

Heinrich Kaupel[31] parted company with his scholarly predecessors in that he denied a progression from Job to Zechariah (or *vice versa*) and in that he examined the uses of *śāṭān* outside of Job, Zechariah, and Chronicles.[32] He concluded that *śāṭān* means "enemy," not "accuser," and stated that if Zechariah had wanted to convey the meaning "accuser" he could have used the term *ʾîš rîb*.[33] As we shall see, 2 Sam 19:23 and Ps 109:6 definitely establish that the noun *śāṭān* could mean "legal accuser" in the terrestrial sphere, and the Ugaritic texts have enabled us to recognize that the Near Eastern concept of a heavenly assembly functioning as a judiciary body is present also in the biblical texts. Kaupel also asserted that *śāṭān* in 1 Chr 21:1 is not a proper name,[34] a conclusion with which the present study agrees. However, Kaupel went on to say that this *śāṭān* was a human agitator.[35]

In 1935, Albert Brock-Unte[36] proposed, as Marti had done, to look for a historical situation that

----

31. *Die Dämonen im Alten Testament* (Augsberg: Dr. Benno Filser, 1930).

32. *Die Dämonen*, 100-102.

33. *Die Dämonen*, 100-101.

34. *Die Dämonen*, 104.

35. *Die Dämonen*, 106-108.

36. "Der Feind: Das alttestamentliche Satansgestalt im Lichte der sozialen Verhältnisse des nahen Orients," *Klio* 28 (1935) 219-227.

could have generated the Satan figure. He lit upon the Amarna letters, specifically those in which vassal kings were being accused of infidelity. He observed that the persons doing the accusing were often rebels, trying to play the great king off against his vassal rulers.[37] Noting that the term <u>śāṭān</u> is used to describe both Hadad and Rezon in 1 Kings 11, Brock-Unte concluded that the term <u>śāṭān</u> belonged to the realm of politics, and meant "opponent in war of a (minor) prince."[38] Stating that Palestine virtually throughout its history fell under the sway of Egyptian or Mesopotamian domination, and given the Amarna evidence that the petty rulers of Palestine had to worry about being slandered at the Egyptian court, Brock-Unte inferred that Israelite leaders must also have been dependent on the goodwill of the rulers of the great nations and, conversely, fearful of the loss of benevolence through slanderous reports.[39]

Aside from the issue that the Palestine of the Amarna period was characterized by the vassal city-state (as opposed to the often independent nation-states of monarchic Israel and Judah), the major problem with Brock-Unte's reconstruction is that he did not precisely circumscribe the source of his analogy. Rather than identifying the source of the analogy as, specifically, the accusation, Brock-Unte transposed into the celestial sphere the entire political context in which these

----

37. "Der Feind," 221-222.

38. "Die Feind," 222-223. On this point, and in his analysis of the use of <u>śāṭān</u> in the psalms, Brock-Unte demonstrates dependence on Harris Birkeland (<u>Die Feinde des Individuums in der israelitischen Psalmenliteratur</u> [Oslo: Grøndahl and Sons, 1933] 86, 203).

39. "Die Feind," 222.

accusations took place. As a result, his reconstruction does not explain, for instance, Num 22:22-35, in which the mal'āk yhwh who comes forth lĕśāṭān certainly cannot be described as a rebel prince.[40]

Proceeding, as we shall see, on the basis of a spurious etymology, N. H. Tur-Sinai[41] suggested that the noun śāṭān originally meant "the one who goes to and fro,"[42] and that therefore Satan was patterned after a court official whose duty it was to patrol his overlord's empire and report any untoward behavior.[43] If this secret agent could find no fault, he sometimes resorted to provoking crimes (// 1 Chr 21:1).[44] Tur-Sinai's thesis was reviewed by Adolphe Lods,[45] who criticized the etymological argument upon which the thesis was based[46] but nevertheless accepted Tur-Sinai's proposal in the limited sense of agreeing that the śāṭān of Job was modelled on a secret-police agent.[47] After reviewing the process of law in Israel, Egypt and Mesopotamia, Lods concluded that there was no office of public

----

40. So also Kluger, Satan, 15.

41. "How Satan Came into the World," Expository Times, 1936/7. Tur-Sinai's views were later incorporated into his Job commentary (The Book of Job: A New Commentary [Jerusalem: Kiryath Sepher, 1957] 38-45).

42. Job, 41.

43. Job, 42.

44. Job, 43.

45. Les origines de la figure de satan: ses fonctions à la cour céleste," Mélanges syriens offerts à Monsieur René Dussaud (Paris: Geuthner, 1939) vol. 2, 649-660.

46. "Les origines," 658.

47. "Les origines," 656, 658.

prosecutor.[48] Indeed, as we shall see, there does not seem to have been a royal (or local) official whose duties approximated those of a public prosecutor or attorney general. From this, Lods drew the conclusion that the *śāṭān* of Zechariah 3 is not the celestial equivalent of a public prosecutor, but rather a "personnage indéterminé."[49] Again, this is quite possibly correct. Lods concluded by stating that we cannot establish whether the *śāṭān* of Job predates the *śāṭān* of Zechariah or whether the reverse is the case, and therefore the origin of Satan remains obscure.[50]

As mentioned above, Rivkah Kluger published in 1948 a work entitled "Die Gestalt des Satans im Alten Testament," which was translated into English and published in 1967 as *Satan in the Old Testament*. I have already discussed the developmental orientation of her work. Although the English version of her study significantly postdates the influence that the discoveries at Ugarit had on identifying the divine council image in Israelite thought, Kluger's book takes virtually no note of the vast literature that has been generated concerning the role of the divine council as a judiciary body.[51]

----

48. "Les origines," 651-655.

49. "Les origines," 659.

50. "Les origines," 660.

51. For instance, in her lengthy chapter dealing with the *bĕnê hāʾĕlōhîm* (pp. 79-136), Kluger refers to Ugarit only twice. She mentions the gods *šhr* [sic] and *šlm* (p. 116, n.76), and states that the myths of the fall of the angels and the victory over the sea monster are evidenced at Ugarit (p. 116, n. 77). She does, however, note that there was a Babylonian heavenly accuser figure (pp. 135-136).

The only major work since Kluger to discuss *śāṭān* in the Old Testament is Herbert Haag's *Teufelsglaube*.[52] For Haag, Yahweh's heavenly court was composed of "demoted" Canaanite deities;[53] Yahweh's acquisition of a heavenly court, including the office of Accuser, was a post-exilic phenomenon.[54] These statements are simply wrong. The developmental approach is still in evidence; for Haag, Zechariah is the most primitive text,[55] and Job is more advanced because, since God's growing omnipotence rendered the post of Accuser redundant, the *śāṭān*'s role expanded beyond those boundaries and the character became more malicious.[56] In 1 Chronicles, Satan is given independent existence as the embodiment of God's anger.[57]

There has been one thread running through the modern study of *śāṭān* that I have not yet mentioned. In 1902, H. Zimmern[58] proposed comparing the *śāṭān* of Job and Zechariah to the Mesopotamian figure of the *bēl dabābi*. Just as humankind had helper deities, they also had deities who accused them.[59] As we shall see, the

----

52. Tübingen: Katzmann, 1974. Karl Frick's *Das Reich Satans* (Graz: Akademische Druck-U., 1982) devotes 12 pages to *śāṭān* in the Old Testament, of which 9 pages are direct quotes, primarily from Roskoff and Kluger.

53. *Teufelsglaube*, 164, 200.

54. *Teufelsglaube*, 199.

55. *Teufelsglaube*, 201.

56. *Teufelsglaube*, 204.

57. *Teufelsglaube*, 214.

58. *Die Keilinschriften und das Alte Testament*[3] (Berlin: Reuther und Reichard, 1902) vol. 2, 463.

59. *Keilinschriften*, 461.

term *bēl dabābi* provides one of several good parallels to the Hebrew noun *śāṭān*. Working from a different point of departure (viz. the figure of the Paraclete), Sigmund Mowinckel[60] and Nils Johansson[61] demonstrated that the book of Job envisaged the figure of a favorable divine witness, a *mal⁾āk* or *mēlîṣ*, who could intercede in front of God on behalf of a suffering human being. The present study accepts these observations as correct, and brings them into sharper focus by placing them within the context of the divine assembly as judiciary body.

The present study makes no attempt to identify the origins of Satan; if anything, we must divest ourselves of the notion of Satan if we are to accurately perceive how the noun *śāṭān* functions in each of the passages under examination. As we shall see, the noun *śāṭān* could mean both "adversary" in general and "legal accuser" in particular, and it was used to refer to various beings both terrestrial and divine when they played either of these adversarial roles. Proceeding from this observation, it becomes clear that there is not one celestial *śāṭān* in the Hebrew Bible, but rather the potential for many. And if the *śāṭān* of, for instance, Zechariah 3 is not the same *śāṭān* as the one dispatched to oppose Balaam nor the one who provoked David to number Israel, then we certainly should not speak of a single, developing character or personality. To do so would be to speak from within the worldview of our pre-critical Jewish and Christian predecessors.

----

60. "Hiob's gō⁾ēl und Zeuge im Himmel," Karl Budde (ed.), *Vom Alten Testament* (Giessen: Alfred Töpelmann, 1925) 207-212 (=*BZAW* 41); "Die Vorstellungen des Spätjudentums vom heiligen Geist als Fürsprecher und die johanneische Paraklet," *ZNW* 32 (1933) 97-130.

61. *Parakletoi* (Lund: Gleerup, 1940).

Chapter 2

THE ETYMOLOGY OF *śāṭān*

In this section, I shall first establish the primitive radicals of the noun *śāṭān* in order to delimit the pool of etymologically related noun and verb forms in both Hebrew and the cognate languages. The discussion will focus on establishing whether the -*ān* at the end of *śāṭān* is suffixal,[1] or whether the *nûn* should be considered a root consonant. Although seemingly trivial, the point is an important one because, if the *nûn* is denied status as a root consonant, then the noun *śāṭān* may be etymologically related to one of several geminate, third weak, and hollow verbs. On the semantic level, these potential cognates are tantalizing. They include "to stray,"[2] "to revolt/fall away,"[3] "be unjust,"[4] "burn,"[5] and "seduce."[6] Indeed, both ancient and modern

----

1. Hans Bauer and Pontus Leander, *Historische Grammatik der Hebräischen Sprache des Alten Testaments* (Halle: Niemeyer, 1918-1922; reprinted Hildesheim: Georg Olms, 1962) vol. 1, section 61tθ; N. H. Tur-Sinai, *The Book of Job* (Jerusalem: Kiryath Sepher, 1957) 42. Gerhard von Rad ("*diabolos*," *TDNT* vol. 2, 73) notes that it is debated whether *śāṭān* is a simple *qāṭāl* form, or whether -*ān* is suffixal.

2. Arabic *šṭṭ*, Hebrew *śṭh*, Ethiopic *šṭy*, Akkadian *šâṭu* 1 and Syriac *sṭʾ*.

3. Aramaic *swṭ*, Mandaean *swṭ*, and Hebrew *śwṭ*.

4. Arabic *šṭṭ*.

5. Syriac *swṭ* and Arabic *šyṭ*.

6. Ethiopic *šṭy* and Hebrew *śṭh*.

etymologists have listed the noun *śāṭān* under one or another of these verbal roots.[7] It is important, therefore, to establish whether *nûn* is a root consonant. In order to do so, I shall outline what various Semitists have written concerning the -*ān* suffix, and then discuss their observations specifically in terms of the noun *śāṭān*.

The Semitic languages evidence a suffix *-*ān* which, when appended to a nominal base, creates an abstact noun, an adjective, or a diminutive.[8] In Hebrew, the afformative *-*ān* should be and usually is realized as -*ôn* as a consequence of having undergone the Canaanite shift. However, there are a significant number of cases in which the shift apparently did not take place. Grammarians have posited several reasons why this atypical -*ān* might occur in Hebrew. There has been consensus with regard to two causes: Aramaic loanwords,[9]

----

7. For instance, according to E. W. Lane (*An Arabic-English Lexicon* [London: Williams and Norgate, 1872] book 1, part 4, 1552, 1631), Arab grammarians could not agree whether *šayṭān* should be listed under *šṭn*, "be remote (from the mercy of God)," or *šyṭ* "to burn." E. S. Drower and R. Macuch (*A Mandaic Dictionary* [Oxford: Clarendon, 1963] 324) list the Mandaean equivalent of *śāṭān* (*saṭana*) under third weak *sṭa*, "turn aside, stray."

8. Paul Joüon, *Grammaire de l'hébreu biblique* (Rome: Pontifical Biblical Institute, 1923) section 88M a-f; S. Moscati, *An Introduction to the Comparative Grammar of the Semitic Languages* (Wiesbaden: Harrassowitz, 1964) 82. C. Brockelmann (*Grundriss der vergleichenden Grammatik der semitischen Sprachen* [Berlin: Reuther und Reichard, 1908] vol. 1, section 216) added local endings to the list of functions. Joüon preferred to treat local endings separately (section 91h).

9. Joüon (*Grammaire*, section 88M c) cited *ʾabdān* and *ʿinyān*. Bauer and Leander (*Historische Grammatik*, vol. 1, section 61oθ) cited *ʿinyān* and *binyān*.

and vowel dissimilation.[10] These two categories, however, are not sufficient to explain all Hebrew nouns evidencing the suffix *-ān*. Bauer and Leander[11] claimed that some of these maverick nouns belonged to an early layer of the Hebrew language, but they do not demonstrate why this would have encouraged retention of **-ān*. Moscati[12] considered the possibility that proto-Semitic had more than one **-ān* suffix, and stated that the **-ān* atypically retained in Hebrew perhaps could be attributed to an originally distinct morpheme.

Of the three categories of meaning generally associated with **-ān*, namely abstract noun, adjective, and diminutive, none accurately describes the noun *śāṭān*. Furthermore, among the conditions proposed to explain the retention of **-ān* in certain Hebrew words, none applies to the noun *śāṭān*. In terms of a general linguistic discussion, therefore, I see no tenable reason for hypothesizing that *śāṭān* is composed of a base plus *-ān* suffix.

Both Tur-Sinai[13] and Bauer and Leander[14] pointed to Arabic in support of their contention that that the *-ān* of *śāṭān* is a suffix. The Arabic equivalent of *śāṭān* is *šayṭān*, which the aforementioned scholars

----

10. That is, *-ôn* is avoided when the preceding syllable contains a *u* or *o* vowel, for example, *šulḥān* and *qorbān*. Cf. Joüon, *Grammaire*, section 88M d; Bauer and Leander, *Historische Grammatik*, vol. 1, section 61mθ; Brockelmann, *Grundriss*, vol. 1, section 210.

11. *Historische Grammatik*, vol. 1, 61bθ.

12. *Comparative Grammar*, 82.

13. *Job*, 43.

14. *Historische Grammatik*, vol. 1, section 61tθ.

took as evidence for derivation from a primitive hollow root plus suffix. Bauer and Leander[15] proposed either *śwṭ* or *śyṭ*, yet Hebrew middle weak roots are not categorically incapable of taking the suffix -*ôn*.[16] If the root is *śwṭ* or *śyṭ*, how then should we account for -*ān* rather than -*ôn*? Furthermore, *qayṭāl* is a perfectly acceptable nominal pattern in Arabic,[17] and therefore one need not infer from the form *šayṭān* that the *yōd* must be taken as part of the root. Thus comparison with Arabic offers no compelling reason to analyze *śāṭān* as base plus suffix -*ān*.

Tur-Sinai[18] explained the alleged retention of *-*ān* (that is, -*ān* rather than -*ôn*) by claiming that *śāṭān* "...returned [!] to Hebrew in the form *saṭan* [sic] from one of the related dialects." Tur-Sinai's vagueness bespeaks the fact that he could offer no hard evidence to back up his assertion. In addition, Tur-Sinai claimed that the primitive root was *šwṭ*; he justified the initial sibilant on the basis that biblical Hebrew did not differentiate graphically between *śîn* and *šîn*.[19] In the case of biblical Hebrew, however, graphic non-differentiation of *śîn* and *šîn* does not imply phonemic equivalence. Tur-Sinai's proposition neglects the fact that the Hebrew alphabet was borrowed from the Phoenicians and therefore was not necessarily suited to represent the phonemes of Hebrew on a one-to-one basis.

----

15. *Historische Grammatik*, vol. 1, section 61tθ.

16. For example, *śāśôn*, *lāṣôn*, and *zādôn* (Joüon, *Grammaire*, 88M b).

17. Lane, *Lexicon*, book 1, part 4, 1552.

18. *Job*, 42.

19. Tur-Sinai, *Job*, 42.

Furthermore, if **ś* and **š* had merged in biblical Hebrew it would have been an unconditioned merger, and it would contravene linguistic law for these two phonemes to unmerge in the Masoretic system. In short, Tur-Sinai's proposal to derive *śāṭān* from *šwṭ* may be dismissed.

In summary, the above review of evidence and arguments demonstrates that there is no compelling reason to argue that the noun *śāṭān* is composed of a base plus -*ān* suffix. The *nûn*, therefore, must be part of the root, and the nominal pattern is a simple *qāṭāl*.

If, as it has been demonstrated, *nûn* is part of the root, what should we make of the fact that a variety of geminate, third weak, and hollow verbs in various Semitic languages[20] are, on the semantic level, such tantalizing potential cognates because they carry meanings that are strikingly appropriate to the character and function of Satan? Although Tur-Sinai's arguments have been shown to be erroneous, his reason for deriving *śāṭān* from the verb *šwṭ* throws light on this question. Tur-Sinai observed that, in Job 1:7 and 2:2, the *śāṭān*'s activity is described by the verb *šwṭ*.[21] Although his proposal to derive *śāṭān* from the verb *šwṭ* violates modern etymological principles, the author of Job may very well have chosen the verb *šwṭ* to describe the activity of the Joban *śāṭān* under the influence of folk-etymological tradition.[22] From aetiological stories such as the naming of Cain (Gen 4:1, *qyn* and *qnh*) and the tower of Babel (Gen 11:1-9, *bbl* and *bll*), we know that

----

20. See notes 2-6.

21. Tur-Sinai, *Job*, 41.

22. So also Kluger, *Satan*, 31.

the ancient writers of the Hebrew Bible delighted in explaining the names of key persons, places, and other noteworthy items by associating them with another word or phrase that had a clear, and relevant, meaning. Although we, from our modern vantage point, can disavow the relationship between a word and its folk derivation, the relationship was archaically felt to be a valid one and hence had the potential for impact and import. This is true not only within the corpus of the Hebrew Bible itself,[23] but can be demonstrated within the deuterocanonical corpus,[24] in the New Testament,[25] and in Talmudic and midrashic literature.[26] Thus I suggest that although the noun śāṭān has no strict derivational relationship to the various roots cited at the beginning of this chapter, the semantic correspondences are not coincidental. Although it is beyond the scope of this investigation to explore these relationships, I would conjecture that the semantic correspondences are the result of an interaction between folk-etymological speculation and developing tradition.

Having explained why, in the case of śāṭān, etymologically unrelated roots might exhibit semantic

----

23. Cf., for example, Burke O. Long ("Etymological Etiology and the DT Historian," CBQ 31 [1969] 35-41).

24. See, for example, Jub. 4:15, which places the descent of "the watchers" to earth during the lifetime of Jared (yrd "go down;" compare Gen 5:15-20).

25. For example, Heb 7:2 interprets "Melchizedek" (Gen 14:7-21; Psa 110:4) to mean "king of righteousness." In terms of strict etymology, the name most likely meant "[the god] Ṣedeq is my king." Cf. M. Delcor, "Melchizedek from Genesis to the Qumran Texts and the Epistle to the Hebrews," JSJ 2 (1971) 115-135.

26. Cf., for example, F. Zimmermann, "Folk Etymology of Biblical Names," VTSup 15 (1965) 311-326.

correspondences, let us turn in search of archaic cognates.[27] Investigation of Semitic inscriptional and textual remains that are contemporary with or prior to the Hebrew Bible yields no evidence of cognates. Koehler-Baumgartner's lexicon (p. 918) cites an alleged Akkadian _šaṭānu_, "attack ?".[28] It is incorrect. A verb with this meaning does not exist, and the forms to which Koehler-Baumgartner refers are Št lexical participles of the verb _etēmu/etēnu_.[29] Arabic _šaṭana_ ("to be remote," "to block the way") is certainly cognate, although any attempt to establish the primitive meaning of Hebrew _śāṭān_ on the basis of the Arabic root must be dismissed as methodologically unsound,[30] and the Arabic root is unattested during the period under consideration.

----

27. Having established that _nûn_ is part of the root, the first two consonants are not problematic. Hebrew _ś_ demonstrates a one-to-one correspondence with proto-Semitic *_ś_, as does Hebrew _ṭ_ with proto-Semitic *_ṭ_.

28. Cf. K. L. Tallqvist, _Akkadische Götterepitheta_ (New York: Georg Olms, 1974) 240, 337, 393. Tallqvist posits parsing two forms as Gt participles of _šaṭānu_.

29. _AHW_, 260.

30. James Barr, _The Semantics of Biblical Language_ (London: Oxford University, 1961) 16.

Chapter 3

THE MEANING OF *śāṭān*

The purpose of this section is first to establish the meaning of *śāṭān* in the five contexts (1 Sam 29; 2 Sam 19; 1 Kgs 5, 11; Ps 109) which speak not of celestial satans, but of earthly ones. Next, I will discuss the process of law in Israelite society in so far as it affects our understanding of the term *śāṭān*. Various attempts to establish the existence of professional accusers in Assyria, Babylonia and Persia will be discussed, and finally I will turn to the topic of whether the use of the definite article with *śāṭān* in Job 1-2 and Zechariah 3 indicates that these sources envisaged a post or office of accuser in the divine council.

In 1 Sam 29:4, the noun *śāṭān* simply means "adversary." In this chapter, the Philistines are mustering in preparation for battle against Saul. When David and his troops pass in review before the Philistine commanders, they object to David's participation in the upcoming combat on the basis that David would become an adversary (*śāṭān*), turning against them on the battlefield in order to ingratiate himself to Saul.

In 2 Sam 19:17-24 (RSV vv 16-23), David is en route to Jerusalem after the rebellion of Absalom had been successfully put down. Shimei, a Saulide who had cursed David on his initial flight from Jerusalem (2 Sam 16:5-8), meets David and his entourage at the Jordan with the purpose of seeking legal pardon for his crime of cursing the king. Abishai, a member of the royal court, insists that Shimei should be put to death for cursing Yahweh's anointed. To this, David responds by calling Abishai a *śāṭān*. Given the clearly forensic context of both Shimei's plea for pardon and Abishai's formal charge against him,[1] *śāṭān* is best understood here to mean "legal accuser."[2] Note that Abishai, a member of the royal court, assumes the role of accuser in this specific situation and that therefore the term *śāṭān* does not designate an office, but rather is a function that Abishai performs. Note also that Abishai's accusation is completely justified; Shimei did in fact curse David. Hence *śāṭān* here has no slanderous connotation.

1 Kings 5:16-20 (RSV 5:2-6) presents us with a message sent by Solomon to Hiram, king of Tyre requesting skilled laborers to assist in the temple-building project. Solomon states that David was unable to build a temple for Yahweh because he was engaged in numerous battles against the surrounding peoples. To Solomon, however, Yahweh has given peace; there is no *śāṭān*, and therefore Solomon is able to undertake the building project. Again in this passage *śāṭān* means "adversary," and like 1 Samuel 29 the context is military.

The next context in which the term *śāṭān* is used of human beings is 1 Kings 11. At the beginning of that chapter we are told about Solomon's many foreign

----

1. Cf. H. J. Boecker, *Redeformen des Rechtsleben im alten Testament* (Neukirchen-Vluyn: Neukirchener, 1964) 78-79, 109-110.

2. David's response (v 23a) reads, "How does it concern you, you sons of Zeruiah, that you are becoming today an accuser on my behalf?" Cf. Peggy L. Day, "Abishai the *śāṭān* in 2 Sam 19:17-24," *CBQ* 49 (1987) 543-547.

wives who, when Solomon had grown old, turned his heart away from Yahweh (vv 1-6). As a result of this apostasy it is announced that Yahweh will tear the kingdom out of Solomon's hands, all but one tribe (vv 9-13). Yahweh raises up Hadad of Edom as a *śāṭān* against Solomon (v 14) as well as Rezon in Damascus in the same capacity (vv 23, 25). How exactly Hadad affects Solomon is unclear. The story breaks off abruptly; perhaps verse 25b originally followed verse 22, and MT's *ʾărām* should be emended to read "Edom." This would mean that Hadad regained some[3] control over Edom. Rezon captured Damascus (v 24) and harassed Israel all Solomon's days (v 25a).

1 Kings 5 and 11 must be set within the Deuteronomistic understanding of history as a vehicle through which divine judgment is expressed. Dtr^1's[4] overall structuring of the reign of Solomon is a case in point. After ridding himself of royal rivals and other nuisances and thus establishing his grip on the kingdom (1 Kgs 2), Solomon settles into a reign of peace and prosperity. As an introduction to his reign, it is stated (1 Kgs 3:3) that Solomon kept the covenant stipulations of Yahweh, and thus the theological ground is established for a period of stability and prosperity (1 Kgs 5:4-5, RSV 4:24-25). Indeed, it is not until Solomon's old age, when he is portrayed as being corrupted by the worship imported by his foreign wives

----

3. Cf. John Bright, *A History of Israel* (London: SCM, 1966) 183.

4. This study accepts the analysis of the editions of the Deuteronomistic history proposed by F. M. Cross (*Canaanite Myth and Hebrew Epic* [Cambridge: Harvard University, 1973] 274-289).

(1 Kgs 11:1-8) that the purported tranquility[5] is broken. Because Solomon had done evil in the eyes of the Lord (1 Kgs 11:6), Hadad and Rezon were raised up[6] by Yahweh to harass Solomon. While Solomon had remained faithful to Yahweh, there had been no *śāṭān* to disturb his peaceful reign (1 Kgs 5:18, RSV 5:4).

Although noting that *śāṭān* in 1 Kings 5 and 11 may simply be translated "adversary," Gerhard von Rad[7] has suggested that there also may be a legal dimension to the Deuteronomist's use of the term in these two chapters. Solomon had sinned, and because of this sin

----

5. The artificiality of the construct that peace and prosperity emanate from covenant fidelity, and are replaced by political insurgency as the price of forsaking the worship of Yahweh, is perhaps betrayed by the statement in 1 Kgs 11:25 that Rezon, at least, harried Israel *all* the days of Solomon's life. Note also that Hadad is portrayed as returning to Edom in response to hearing that David and Joab were dead (1 Kgs 11:21), which again might imply that his agitation against Solomon began early in Solomon's reign.

To my knowledge, there is no independent data by which to establish at what point in Solomon's reign Hadad and Rezon began challenging Israelite sovereignty. Those scholars who tend to go along with the biblical record cite the necessity of requisite time to accumulate wealth (Wayne Pitard, "Ancient Damascus: A Historical Study of the Syrian City-State from Earliest Times until its Fall to the Assyrians in 732 B.C.E.," Ph.D. dissertation, Harvard University, 1982, 143-145), the decadence engendered by said wealth (M. Unger, *Israel and the Arameans of Damascus* [Grand Rapids: Zondervan, 1957] 54), and the rise of the vigorous twenty-second dynasty of Egypt (A. Malamat, "Aspects of the Foreign Policies of David and Solomon," *JNES* 22 (1963) 17) as reasons for affirming that Solomon was not pestered by the aforementioned upstarts until late in his reign.

6. Note Dtr[1]'s use of *hēqîm* in his programmatic statement concerning the relationship between Israel's fidelity to Yahweh and the course of Israel's history in Judg 2:18.

7. "*diabolos*," 73.

Yahweh raised up Hadad and Rezon as adversaries against him. Hadad and Rezon are, therefore, according to von Rad, concrete illustations of divine judgment, and thus *śāṭān* has a legal connotation: Hadad and Rezon are accusers of Israel.

Whereas von Rad is certainly correct in stating that the term *śāṭān* has been drawn into the Deuteronomist's legalistic conception of sin and punishment, I question whether it is on this basis correct to characterize Hadad and Rezon as accusers. R. Frankena[8] has noted that one of the typical blessings construed to be a reward for adherence to covenant stipulations is peace. This can be illustrated from within the biblical record by, for instance, 2 Chr 17:3-13. In this passage, Jehoshaphat is described as wholly loyal to Yahweh and covenant law, and as a consequence the kingdoms round about Judah wage no war against him. Conversely, lack of peace is one of the treaty curses invoked for breach of covenant by, for instance, Suppiluliumas[9] and attested to in the biblical record by, for example, 2 Chr 16:7-9. I would suggest, therefore, that the term *śāṭān* had a legal dimension for the Deuteronomist because of the role that peace (or lack of peace) played in the Deuteronomist's understanding of covenant fidelity. When Solomon was loyal to Yahweh, he had no adversaries. When he broke the covenant stipulation that prohibited worshipping other gods, Hadad and Rezon became politico-military enemies. Their role is quasi-forensic because breach of covenant is a legal

----

8. "The Vassal Treaties of Esarhaddon and the Dating of Deuteronomy," *OTS* 14 (1965) 136.

9. A. Goetze, "God Lists, Blessings and Curses of the Treaty Between Suppiluliumas and Kurtiwaza," *ANET*, 206.

transgression, not because they are per se accusers of Israel.

The final context in which śāṭān has a terrestrial referent is Psalm 109. This individual psalm of lament opens with the psalmist's complaint about being baselessly attacked by slanderous enemies (vv 1-5), and moves to an extended curse (vv 6-19) followed by a plea for Yahweh's intervention and blessing (vv 21-22, 26-28), and the promise to praise Yahweh in the congregation (vv 30-31). The major problem posed by Psalm 109 is the abrupt change from a plurality of enemies in verses 1-5 to a single opponent in verses 6-19, followed by a return to the plural in verses 20-31. This shift from the plural to the singular and back to the plural again has led several scholars to argue that verses 1-5 and 20-31 were originally a single compositional unit that has been split apart to include verses 6-19.[10] The noun śāṭān is used in Psalm 109 in the following context:

> 6 Lay a charge of guilt against him, and let an accuser (śāṭān) stand at his right hand.
> 7 When he is judged, let him come forth guilty, and may intercession for him be regarded as a crime.

Those scholars who assert that śāṭān does not mean

----

10. For example, Moses Buttenweiser (The Psalms [Chicago: U. of Chicago, 1939] 742) and Oswald Loretz (Die Psalmen [AOAT 28; Neukirchen-Vluyn: Neukirchener, 1979] Teil 2, 158-159). The further redactional activity identified by these and other scholars does not concern us here. J. H. Eaton (Psalms [London: SCM, 1967] 259) accounts for the shift to the singular in verses 6-19 by positing that a traditional execration formula was being employed. Other commentators (for example, Hermann Gunkel, Die Psalmen [HKAT; Göttingen: Vandenhoeck und Ruprecht, 1926] 478) maintain the compositional integrity of the psalm, but I do not find their arguments convincing.

"accuse" typically explain this passage by noting that Ps 109:3 uses the root <u>lḥm</u>, which sets the context in the arena of war.[11] However, as has been noted above, there is good reason to believe that verses 6-19 are a discrete unit. There seems to me to be little doubt that <u>śāṭān</u> has a forensic connotation in Ps 109:6. Verse 7 clearly states that the psalmist wants his opponent to be brought to justice (<u>bhšpṭw</u>), and the expression "stand on the right hand" (v 6) is also clearly forensic.[12] Again, note that there is no reason to believe that the <u>śāṭān</u>'s sought-for testimony is slanderous.

In his 1968 article entitled "The Eyes of the Lord," A. Leo Oppenheim stated that there is no single interpretation of the noun <u>śāṭān</u> that fits all nine of the contexts in which it is found in the Hebrew Bible.[13] Our survey of the five texts in which <u>śāṭān</u> has a terrestrial referent already bears this statement out. In 1 Samuel 29 <u>śāṭān</u> is used to mean "adversary" without any hint of legal undertones. On the other hand Psalm 109 clearly envisages a formal court hearing in which a <u>śāṭān</u> brings charges against the psalmist's antagonist. It is as fruitless, therefore, to insist that the term is purely legal as it is to propose that it has no forensic connotation whatsoever.

In between the extremes represented by 1 Samuel 29 and Psalm 109, 2 Samuel 19 and 1 Kings 5 and 11 demonstrate that <u>śāṭān</u> can have additional shades of

----

11. For example, Birkeland (<u>Die Feinde</u>, 203).

12. Roland de Vaux, <u>Ancient Israel: Its Life and Institutions</u> (New York: McGraw-Hill, 1961) 156.

13. A. Leo Oppenheim, "The Eyes of the Lord," <u>JAOS</u> 88 (1968) 176.

meaning. Broadly speaking, these shades of meaning are due to the fact that the Israelite conception of what constituted legal process was neither as narrow nor as discrete as the modern, western notion of the process of law.[14] Thus although 2 Sam 19:17-24 lacks a formal court setting, the language and the process are clearly forensic. Executive powers had not been differentiated clearly: David as head of state was also the highest legal official in the land. Thus Abishai's accusation against Shimei is a legal accusation, and Abishai is a *śāṭān* in the sense that he is Shimei's legal adversary.

In that the relationship between Israel and Yahweh was perceived as a contractual (covenant) arrangement, human contravention of the agreement could be expressed in terms of legal offense. The metaphor is so pervasive that Dennis McCarthy[15] has argued that the announcement of divine anger should be understood legalistically. Various calamities, such as plague, famine or warfare on the collective level and sickness, injury or animosity on the personal level were understood as judgment for sin, and thus could be invested with legal overtones. Interpreted in this framework, adversity becomes a sign of legal transgression and calamity acquires forensic force. Hence Hadad and Rezon

----

14. For a general discussion of legal process in traditional societies, see Roberts (*Order and Dispute*) and Bohannan ("Differing Realms"). Roberts (192-197) outlines the problems inherent in studies that proceed from an ethnocentric definition of law, and Bohannan (44) proposes the notion of a zone of transition between that which is unquestionably legal and that which is not.

15. "The Wrath of Yahweh and the Structural Unity of the Deuteronomistic History," J. L. Crenshaw and J. T. Willis (eds.), *Essays in Old Testament Ethics* (New York: Ktav, 1974) 100.

are not simply Solomon's adversaries, they are living proof that Solomon has breached his covenant with Yahweh. In the same way that Job could describe his wizened state as a witness (*ʿēd*) that testifies against him (Job 16:8; cf. Ezek 29:16),[16] so the existence of Hadad and Rezon as successful enemies could be construed as evidence that Solomon had transgressed divine law.

Having discussed the semantic range of the term *śāṭān* in the five contexts in which it has a human referent, let us briefly compare our findings with the texts in which *śāṭān* refers to a heavenly being. In Job 1-2 and Zechariah 3 *śāṭān* clearly has a forensic connotation. Unlike Psalm 109 and 2 Samuel 19, however, *śāṭān* in Job and Zechariah is construed with the definite article, perhaps implying an office of accuser in the heavenly assembly. This topic will be examined below. The messenger of Yahweh dispatched as a *śāṭān* to bar Balaam's way (Num 22) is most closely paralleled by Hadad and Rezon. In both cases, Yahweh's anger (1 Kgs 11:9; Num 22:22) was the direct cause of adversaries being sent out (Num 22) or raised up (1 Kgs 11) to challenge someone who had lost divine favor. The messenger of Yahweh, Hadad and Rezon are all agents of divine anger and, consequently, vehicles of divine judgment. The role of Yahweh's messenger is more explicit, however, in that the messenger not only acts as an adversary in the sense of posing a physical threat but also informs Balaam of the precise reason for Yahweh's anger (Num 22:32). If, as McCarthy[17] has suggested, we understand the announcement of divine wrath as a paralegal expression, then the

----

16. Cf. Lods, "Les origines," 652.

17. "Wrath," 100.

messenger's announcement of the reason for Yahweh's anger is in fact the statement of a legal charge, and Balaam's response (ḥāṭāʾtî, v 34) is a confession of guilt.[18] Thus in Numbers 22 Yahweh's messenger is a śāṭān not only in the general sense of being an adversary, but also in the sense of playing the role of legal accuser at the behest of his sender, Yahweh. The intimate connection between divine wrath and the action of a śāṭān is also evident in 1 Chr 21:1, where wayyaʿămōd śāṭān ʿal-yiśrāʾēl is actually substituted for wayyōsep...ʾap-yhwh laḥărôt bĕyiśrāʾēl (2 Sam 24:1), perhaps implying a functional equivalence of the two phrases.

As mentioned above, in Job 1-2 and Zechariah 3 śāṭān is construed with the definite article. In both passages the context is forensic, and thus śāṭān means "accuser." Does the presence of the definite article indicate that Job 1-2 and Zechariah 3 envisage a specific member of the bĕnê ʾĕlōhîm holding the post or office of accuser? In order to address this question let us first examine Israelite legal practise to determine whether there existed a post or office of legal adversary that could have provided a model for a celestial office of accuser. Next, we shall look toward Assyria and Babylonia in search of a terrestrial analogy and in order to discuss certain Akkadian terms denoting celestial accusers. Finally, we shall turn to the early years of the Persian empire.

In his 1959 article "Das Amt des Mazkir. Zur

----

18. For ḥāṭāʾtî as a stock legal expression acknowledging guilt, see Boecker (Redeformen, 111-114).

Rechtsstruktur des öffentlichen Lebens in Israel,"[19] H. Graf Reventlow argued that the monarchic office of *mazkîr* (2 Sam 8:16, 20:24; 1 Kgs 4:3; 2 Kgs 18:18,37; Isa 36:3,22; 1 Chr 18:15; 2 Chr 34:8) was a legal office, comparable to that of public prosecutor or attorney general. He further stated that *śāṭān* was a term equivalent to *mazkîr*, and that therefore *śāṭān* also meant "public prosecutor." Reventlow based his argument on establishing forensic uses of the verbal root *zkr* in both the qal and hiphil, emphasizing the use of the root in legal accusations.[20] From this examination, Reventlow concluded that the *mazkîr* was the highest legal official in the land, the *Anklagevertreter*.[21] Reventlow claimed that the office had its roots in the period of the amphictyony, at which time the *mazkîr* was the prosecutor of covenant offenses.[22]

Many of Reventlow's examples, especially of *zkr* in the qal, are too general to inspire confidence that *zkr* is being used as a legal-technical term (e.g. Exod 20:8; Num 15:39; Jos 1:13; Ps 103:18; Mal 3:22). However, even when the unpersuasive examples are eliminated, enough documentation remains to support Reventlow's general position (e.g. Isa 43:26; Ps 109:14). But as H. J. Boecker[23] has pointed out, *hizkîr* does not necessarily carry an indictive force: it can be used to

----

19. *TZ* 15 (1959) 161-175.

20. "Das Amt," 164-170.

21. "Das Amt," 172.

22. "Das Amt," 174.

23. H. J. Boecker, "Erwägungen zum Amt des Mazkir," *TZ* 17 (1961) 212-216; *Redeformen des Rechtslebens im Alten Testament* (Neukirchen-Vluyn: Neukirchener, 1964) 108.

describe the action of someone speaking in the accused's favor as well as to his or her detriment. To illustrate this, Boecker points to Gen 40:14, where Joseph asks the *śar hammašqîm* to bring his case to the attention of the pharaoh. As the context makes clear, Joseph expects the action to be beneficial to him. For Boecker, the hiphil of *zkr* describes any person entitled to speak in the judicial assembly standing up to make something known. Within the context of justice at the gate, every citizen had the right to speak for or against the accused, and in this capacity a citizen could be called a *mazkîr*. Extrapolating from the use of *hizkîr lĕṭôbâ* (Neh 5:19, 13:31) and *hizkîr ʿāwōn* (e.g. 1 Kgs 17:18), Boecker speculates that a citizen speaking on the defendant's behalf was called a *mazkîr lĕṭôbâ*, and one speaking against the accused was a *mazkîr ʿāwōn*.[24]

Returning to the monarchic office of *mazkîr*, it should be noted that, with the exception of Reventlow, those who have tackled the problem see no forensic component in this office.[25] Typically, scholars have turned to Egypt in search of an analogy, on the hypothesis that the newly constituted Davidic state structured itself according to Egyptian models.[26] Those

----

24. Boecker, "Erwägungen," 214. The only two uses of the participle *mazkîr* plus *ʿāwōn* are Ezek 21:28 (RSV v. 23) and 29:16, although there are several additional instances of *zkr* in the qal, niphal and hiphil, plus *ʿāwōn*.

25. Any attempt to specify the role of the royal *mazkîr* is highly conjectural. When mentioned in the biblical sources the office completely lacks description.

26. Joachim Begrich, "Sōfēr und Mazkîr," *ZAW* 58 (1940/41) 11-12; Boecker, "Erwägungen," 214; John Bright, "The Organization and Administration of the Israelite State," in F. M. Cross et. al. (eds.), *Magnalia Dei* (New York:

who affirm Egyptian influence most often parallel the mazkîr with the Egyptian wḥmw, "reporter, herald," on the basis that the Egyptian term is the semantic equivalent of mazkîr.[27]

Tryggve Mettinger notes that the LXX translates mazkîr with the term hupomnēmatographos, which was the name of an important government official in Ptolemaic Egypt whose task it was to keep royal diaries or journals.[28] Although this equivalence can by no means be considered decisive evidence for pinpointing the role of the mazkîr, it certainly indicates that the LXX translators did not understand the term in a forensic sense.

In summary, the monarchic office of mazkîr need not be invested with juridical force. Although the verbal root zkr can be demonstrated to have a place in the legal life of ancient Israel, it does not always

----

Doubleday, 1976) 203; R. de Vaux, "Titres et functionnaires égyptiens à la cour de David et de Salomon," RB 48 (1939) 394-395; Tryggve Mettinger, Solomonic State Officials (Lund: Gleerup, 1971) 21-23; A. Soggin, "The Davidic-Solomonic Kingdom," in J. H. Hayes and J. M. Miller (eds.), Israelite and Judaean History (London: SCM, 1977) 358.

27. This is the opinion of all those cited in the above footnote, except Mettinger. D. B. Redford ("Studies in Relations between Palestine and Egypt During the First Millennium B.C.: The Taxation System of Solomon," J. W. Wevers and D. B. Redford [eds.], Studies in the Ancient Palestinian World [Toronto: University of Toronto, 1972] 141-144) does not believe that Egypt supplied the organizational model for the Israelite court, but neither does he think that the office of mazkîr was a judicial one.

28. Mettinger, State Officials, 22.

carry a forensic connotation.[29] When it does, further specification is necessary to determine whether the action is to the benefit or detriment of the accused. Thus the royal *mazkîr*, if understood to describe a judicial office, could not be construed as a public prosecutor because *mazkîr* without further specification is ambiguous as to the actor's relationship to the accused. In addition, both proposed parallels with Egyptian officialdom and the LXX translation of *mazkîr* suggest that the office in ancient Israel was not a judicial one.

When we turn to examine the process of law at the local community level, or "justice at the gate," it is generally acknowledged that there was no office of public prosecutor.[30] The litigants themselves could bring their case before the assembly (Deut 25:1), or witnesses could bring a case to trial (1 Kgs 21:13). The most common general term for "litigant" was *ʾîš rîb*,[31] although this term could also be used more widely to mean simply "disputant," or "someone with a complaint." The strictly technical terms for the litigants seem to have been *baʿal dĕbārîm* (Exod 24:14)[32] and *baʿal mišpāṭ*

----

29. For a good lexical study of *zkr*, see Brevard Childs (*Memory and Tradition in Israel* [Great Britain: W. and J. MacKay and Co., 1962] 9-16).

30. See, for example, H. J. Boecker (*Law and the Administration of Justice in the Old Testament and Ancient Near East* [Minneapolis: Augsburg, 1980] 38) and Roland de Vaux (*Ancient Israel*, 156).

31. Bruce Gemser, "The *Rîb*- or Controversy- Pattern in Hebrew Mentality," VTSup 3 (1955) 123. Gemser also lists less frequent terminology, among which he includes *śāṭān*.

32. H. Zimmern, *Akkadische Fremdwörter als Beweis für babylonische Kultureinfluss* (Leipzig: J. C. Hinrichs, 1914) 24. This term seems to be the Hebrew equivalent of

(Isa 50:8).[33]

From the foregoing review of the evidence, it seems clear that there was no office of accuser in ancient Israel. We can infer from the use of *śāṭān* in 2 Sam 19:24 that any member of the royal court was able to assume the role of accuser; Ps 109:6 is less clear, but again, the particular *śāṭān* mentioned in that passage does not seem to have been a professional accuser, or state prosecutor.

Turning to the Akkadian evidence,[34] Benno Landsberger[35] claimed that, in the Old Babylonian period, the term *munaggirum* designated an office of public accuser, an office that continued in the Middle Babylonian period under the name *ākil karṣī*. His argument, based on the presence of *munaggirum* in vocabularies such as the Old Babylonian lú Series List, has failed to convince other scholars. Thus A. Leo Oppenheim[36] maintains that both *munaggirum* and *ākil karṣī* refer to occasional informers, and that no office of accuser existed until the Neo-Babylonian period.

Akkadian *bēl dabābi*, which can also mean "adversary in court." Von Soden (*AHW*, vol. 1, 146) refers to Hebrew *dibbēr* and Akkadian *dabābu* as cognates, but see the remarks of Stephen Kaufman (*The Akkadian Influences on Aramaic* [Chicago: University of Chicago, 1974] 42).

33. Kaufman (*Akkadian Influences*, 43) suggests that *baᶜal mišpāṭ* is an early calque of Akkadian *bēl dīni*, a common term for "adversary in court" in Neo-Babylonian and Neo-Assyrian.

34. For the following discussion of the Akkadian evidence, I am indebted to William Moran.

35. "Remarks on the Archive of the Soldier Ubarum," *JCS* 9 (1955) 123-124.

36. "The Eyes," 177.

Oppenheim's own claim that certain persons termed *muraššû* and referred to in administrative documents of temple archives should be understood as professional accusers[37] has also been rejected.[38] In short, no one has as yet succeeded in establishing the existence of an office of public prosecutor at any time in Assyro-Babylonian history.

Although, as we have seen, the ancient Semitic languages evidence no cognate for the noun *śāṭān*, there are functional parallels. One of these parallels, the Akkadian term *bēl dabābi*, "adversary, accuser," has already been mentioned. As H. Zimmern[39] observed, *bēl dabābi* could be used to refer both to human legal opponents and accusing deities. Another Akkadian term for a legal accuser, *bēl dīni*, could also be applied to the gods. From the Neo-Assyrian period comes a text[40] that adjures Aššur and Šamaš to be the legal adversaries (*EN di-ni-[šu]*) of whoever should break a certain contractual agreement. Likewise, Nanay and Mār-Bīti are charged to guarantee an agreement sworn in their names; should anyone try to alter the agreement, these two deities were to assume the role of legal adversaries

----

37. Oppenheim, "The Eyes," 178.

38. See *CAD* (M/2, 218), which lists *muraššû*, "slanderer," with no reference to the texts cited by Oppenheim, and the entry *murašû* (*CAD* M/2, 219), "meaning uncertain," with reference to one of the texts cited by Oppenheim.

39. *Keilinschriften*, vol. 2, 461. Zimmern points especially to Maqlû 1:79ff; cf. I. Tzvi Abusch, "Studies in the History of Interpretation of Some Akkadian Incantations and Prayers," (Ph.D. dissertation, Harvard University, 1972) 152-167.

40. ADD (= C. H. Johns, *Assyrian Deeds and Documents*) 780.12, quoted in *CAD*, vol. D, 155.

(*EN.ME di-ni-šu*).[41] Finally, attention may be drawn to the term *ākil karṣī*, yet another term for an accuser.[42] The goddess Ṣarpānītum is described[43] as *ākilat karṣū ṣābitat abbūtu*, "one who accuses and intercedes favorably." Thus although Akkadian does not provide a cognate for Hebrew *śāṭān*, it does provide terms denoting legal opponents that, like *śāṭān*, can be applied both in the terrestrial and celestial spheres. Note that various deities could play the role of accuser, and that one and the same deity could intercede either favorably or unfavorably.[44]

The Akkadian evidence presented in the above paragraph accords well with Job 33:23-25. In this passage, which will be treated at greater length in

----

41. VAS 1 (= Vorderasiatische Schriftdenkmäler der Königlichen Museen zu Berlin) 36 iii.4, quoted in *CAD*, vol. D, 156.

42. As a text treated by P. Kyle McCarter ("Rib-Adda's Appeal to Aziru [*EA* 162, 1-21]," *OrAnt* 12 [1973] 17) clearly demonstrates, *karṣī akālu* need not mean "slander." *EA* 162 is a letter from the Egyptian court to Aziru of Amurru in which the pharaoh upbraids Aziru for failing to report overtures made to him by Rib-Adda of Byblos. Lines 16-17 read, "If you [Aziru] are truly a servant of the king, why did you not denounce him [Rib-Adda] to the king, your lord?" (*šum-ma ÌR ša LUGAL at-tá ki-i ki-i-it-ti am-mì-ni la-a tá-a-ku-ul kar-ṣí-i-šu a-na pa-ni LUGAL EN-ka*). Not only does *karṣī akālu* describe here a legitimate accusation, Aziru is reprimanded for failing to carry out this task. Cf. Samuel Greengus, *Old Babylonian Tablets From Ishchali and Vicinity* (Istanbul: Dutch Historical-Archaeological Inst., 1979) 23.27'-29'; B. Halpern and J. Huehnergard, "El Amarna Letter 252," *Or* 51 (1982) 228-229.

43. F. Thureau-Dangin, *Rituels akkadiens* (Osnabrück: Otto Zeller, 1975) 135, line 258.

44. For additional examples of the judiciary function of the divine assembly from both Mesopotamian and Canaanite texts, see Ackerman ("Psalm 82," 186-205).

chapter 5, Elihu envisages the following scene in the heavenly assembly:

> If he [a man] has a messenger,
> An intermediary, one in a thousand,
> To speak for a human's uprightness,
> Who has mercy on him and says, "Spare him
> from going down to the Pit,
> I have found a ransom."
> Then his flesh becomes fresher than in
> youth,
> He returns to the days of his vigor.

As Mowinckel[45] and Johansson[46] have pointed out, the messenger (*malʾāk*) or intermediary (*mēlîṣ*) is a divine figure who intercedes on behalf of a human being in the heavenly tribunal. Note that this figure could potentially be any member of the council, "one in a thousand."

I have searched in vain for evidence to suggest that professional accusers *per se* existed in the early Persian period. While each satrapy had a secretary or secretaries who communicated directly with the central government[47] and therefore were responsible for reporting seditious activity, I do not think it would be correct to define these people as professional accusers. If we did so, then virtually all highly placed local court officials would have to be defined as professional accusers, and the definition would lose meaning. The ancient witnesses disagree as to whether the Persian monarch employed a "secret service," or whether payment

----

45. "Vorstellungen," 109.

46. *Parakletoi*, 25-26.

47. Seyyed T. Nasr, *Essai sur l'histoire du droit Persan dès l'origine à l'invasion arabe* (Paris: Mechelinck, 1933) 47.

was rendered to incidental informers.[48] Probably both methods of information gathering were utilized. In any event, these people were typically described as "eyes" or "ears" of the king; their impact on the Semitic lexicon can be demonstrated, for instance, by the Aramaic term of office gwškyʾ, which derives from the Old Persian word for "listener."[49]

It seems, therefore, that Job 1-2 and Zechariah 3 present us with a choice. We can affirm that the definite article indicates that the divine assembly had acquired the post of accuser, although we can adduce no certain parallels either from terrestrial judicial terminology or from Canaanite or Mesopotamian mythology. If we adopt this stance, 1 Chr 21:1 indicates that although a post (or posts) of celestial accuser may have been generated, it was still possible for other members of the bĕnê ʾĕlōhîm to play the role of accuser. The other alternative is to understand the definite article to mean "a certain one."[50] Thus it is a certain unspecified accuser who finds fault with Job's piety,[51] and a certain accuser (not necessarily the same one) who challenges the choice of Joshua to be high priest.

----

48. A. Leo Oppenheim, "The Eyes of the Lord," JAOS 88 (1968) 173-174.

49. Oppenheim, "The Eyes," 178.

50. For this meaning of the definite article, see, for example, Joüon (Grammaire, 137m-o).

51. So also Lods, "Les origines," 659.

Chapter 4

śāṭān IN NUMBERS 22:22-35

The first appearance of a heavenly śāṭān to be investigated is found in the story of Balaam and the ass, Num 22:22-35. I have chosen to treat this passage first because it has often been attributed to the J source and therefore viewed as significantly older than the other three passages that this study treats in detail. I will argue that Num 22:22-34[1] stems not from J, but rather has been added by a later hand. I will demonstrate that this conclusion is consistent with information drawn from the recent finds at Deir ᶜAllā as they bear on the biblical Balaam tradition, with an examination of passages outside the Balaam cycle that refer to Balaam, and with current scholarly analysis. The use of śāṭān in Numbers 22 will then be discussed with this conclusion in mind, and finally I will comment upon a textual crux in verse 32.

In the episode of the Balaam cycle told in Num 22:22-35, Balaam has set out with his two attendants on a journey, an act which incurs God's wrath (22:22). God responds by dispatching a messenger, the malʾāk yhwh, described as a śāṭān, who stations himself on the road upon which Balaam is travelling (22:22). Balaam is blissfully ignorant of the sword-wielding messenger, but Balaam's ass sees the danger and avoids the messenger by going off the road and into a field, for which Balaam beats the animal (22:23). The messenger moves further

----

1. Verse 35 is redactional.

along the road and takes up a position in a hollow between two walled vineyards. Balaam's ass once again sees the messenger and presses against one of the walls to avoid him, thus crushing Balaam's foot against one of the walls and earning another beating (22:24-25). Foiled yet again, the mal'āk moves ahead to a place in the road that affords no way to circumvent him; perceiving this, the ass lays down, for which she receives another beating (22:26-27). At this point Yahweh gives the ass the power of speech, and the ass asks Balaam why he has beaten her (v 28). Balaam responds that she has been sporting with him, and that if he had a sword in his hand, he would kill her (v 29). The ass points out that she has been his mount since time immemorial-- has she ever behaved this way before? Balaam admits that she has not (v 30). At this juncture Yahweh uncovers Balaam's eyes so that he can see the sword-wielding messenger standing in the road, and Balaam falls down to the ground (v 31). The messenger asks Balaam why he has struck the ass, and asserts that he has come forth as a śāṭān because Balaam's journey was undertaken hastily (v 32).[2] The ass had seen the messenger and avoided him; had she not done so, the messenger would have killed Balaam (v 33). Balaam then admits his guilt, stating that he did not know that the messenger was standing in the road; if the messenger judges the journey to be wrong, Balaam offers to turn back (v 34). The messenger gives Balaam permission to continue, but adjures him to speak only as instructed. Thus Balaam proceeds with the princes of Balaq (v 35).

As has long been noticed, the episode of Balaam and the ass does not fit unobtrusively into its present

----

2. For a discussion of this crux, see below.

context.[3] Earlier in chapter 22, we read that Balaq the king of Moab had sent messengers[4] to Balaam's homeland[5]

----

3. Walter Gross (Bileam: Literar- und formkritische Untersuchung der Prosa Num 22-24 [München: Kösel, 1974] 419-427) has compiled a comprehensive table of scholars from 1813 through his own study in 1974 who have dealt with the Balaam cycle. According to this table, the ass story was designated obtrusive as early as 1823, by A. G. Hoffman.

4. The identity of these messengers is not stable in the text. Sometimes they are unspecified (22:5), sometimes they are designated as the elders of Moab and Midian (ziqnê môʾāb wĕziqnê midyān, 22:7), and sometimes they are described as the princes (22:13) or servants (22:18) of Balaq, or princes of Moab (22:14, 21). I shall return to this topic below.

5. MT of 22:5a reads: wayyišlaḥ malʾākîm ʾel-bilʿām ben-bĕʿôr pĕtôrâ ʾăšer ʿal-hannāhār ʾereṣ bĕnê-ʿammô liqrōʾ-lô, "And he sent messengers to Balaam son of Beor, to Pethor, which is on the River [=Euphrates], [to] the land of his people, to meet him.". Prior to the finds at Deir ʿAllā, many scholars identified biblical Pethor with Pitru, a town located by Akkadian and Egyptian inscriptional evidence on the river Sagur, a northern tributary of the Euphrates (cf. Gross, Bileam, 103-104.). In light of this identification, W. F. Albright ("The Home of Balaam," JAOS 35 [1917] 389) proposed emending MT ʿmw to ʿdn, because Pitru was located within the district of Bit Adini. However, the subsequent publication by Sidney Smith of the Idrimi inscription caused Albright to reconsider his position ("Some Important Recent Discoveries: Alphabetic Origins and the Idrimi Statue," BASOR 118 [April, 1950] 15-16, n. 13). This inscription evidenced the place name ma-at a-ma-e^{KI}, in northern Syria, and, combining this with Egyptian inscriptional evidence, Albright proposed to read MT ʾrṣ bny ʿmw as "the land of the sons of Amau," in which he located the town of Pitru.

In light of Deir ʿAllā, and with the backing of the Samaritan Pentateuch, LXX, and the Vulgate (although it should be noted that these three texts represent a single textual family within Num 22:22-35), M. Delcor ("Le texte de Deir ʿAllā et les oracles bibliques de Balaʿam," VTSup 32 [1980] 71) has proposed that the primitive reading in Num 22:5 was bĕnê ʿammôn. In addition, he understands MT pĕtôrâ, again with the

to convince him to curse the sons of Israel, who were dwelling opposite him (22:5).[6] These messengers,

----

support of textual witnesses, not as a place name but rather as a designation of Balaam as a dream interpreter. (Cf. BH *ptr*, "interpret," Gen 40-41. Delcor, "Le texte," 64-65 and "Balaʿam Pâtôrâh, 'interprète de songes' au pays d'Ammon, d'après Num 22:5: les témoignages épigraphiques parallèls," *Semitica* 32 [1982] 89-91.) Delcor regards Balaam as an Ammonite because Deir ʿAllā, located near the Jabbok river and hence in the traditional territory of Ammon, makes mention of *blʿm brbʿr*, i.e. Balaam son of Beor. (For the transliterated text of the Deir ʿAllā materials, see Jo Ann Hackett, *The Balaam Text from Deir ʿAllā* [HSM 31; Chico: Scholars Press, 1984] 25-26.) Additionally, it should be noted that the Deir ʿAllā text is written in the Ammonite script tradition (Hackett, *Balaam*, 10, 18-19). This *blʿm brbʿr* is visited in the night by the gods and sees a vision (*wyʾtw.ʾlwh ʾlhn.blylh.wyḥz.mḥzh*; combination 1.1, following the text of Hackett, *Balaam*, 25), which information leads Delcor to propose the reading "dream interpreter" in place of the Masoretic reading.

Both Albright's and Delcor's proposals have inherent weaknesses. Albright's reading of the place name "Amau" for MT *ʿmw* is problematic because what little information we have regarding this place name comes from the sixteenth and fifteenth centuries B.C., and does not provide us with a precise location (Gross, *Bileam*, 111-112; cf. Michael Coogan, "Canaanite Origins and Lineage: Reflections on the Religion of Ancient Israel," P. D. Miller, P. D. Hanson, and S. D. McBride [eds.], *Ancient Israelite Religion: Essays in Honor of Frank Moore Cross* [Philadelphia: Fortress, 1987] 116). As attractive as Delcor's hypothesis is in light of Deir ʿAllā, it fails to account for the tradition, preserved in one of the Balaam oracles (Num 23:7), that Balaam hailed from Aram. Furthermore, the Deir ʿAllā text may itself suggest that Balaam was an Aramean, judging from the fact his patronymic *brbʿr* contains the Aramean word for "son," *bir* (Hackett, *Balaam*, 128). Delcor's suggestion that MT *ptwrh* be read "dream interpreter" is, once again, in light of Deir ʿAllā, attractive, but fails to account for MT's directive *hē*.

6. Although, for P, the incident that occasioned Balaam's action took place on one of the stages of Israel's journey from Sinai to the plains of Moab, the use of the verb *yšb* may indicate that epic tradition envisaged

variously described but clearly prestigious, are replaced in 22:22 by mere attendants (<u>nĕʿārāyw</u>). Even more glaring, in verses 20-21 Balaam is visited by God during the night and instructed by God to go with the men who had come to fetch him, and so he gets up the next morning and rides off with the princes of Moab. Yet in verse 22 we learn that God is angered by Balaam's departure. And to further complicate matters, the <u>malʾāk</u> whom God dispatches to thwart Balaam's progress does not ultimately function to force Balaam homeward, but instead permits the journey (v 35) with virtually the same stipulation as that voiced by God in verse 20.[7] Thus it is obvious that verses 22-35 do not belong to the same source as verses 2-21.

In the classic division of sources represented, for example, by Wellhausen and Carpenter-Battersby, Num 22:22-34 is assigned to J, and verse 35 is a redactional element added to better align the ass story with its surrounding context.[8] 22:1 is also considered redactional, and 22:2-21 is either considered to be E or a blending of JE material.[9] Verse 36 then resumes the (J)E account.

"Israel" actually dwelling in the Trans-Jordan (Martin Noth, <u>Numbers</u> [OTL; London: SCM, 1968] 172).

7. In verse 20 Balaam is instructed to do (<u>ʿśh</u>) as he is told, whereas in verse 35 he is cautioned to speak (<u>dbr</u>) as he is told. Does this slight difference imply that, in the mind of the redactor, the ass story functioned in part to further circumscribe Balaam's activity?

8. See, most conveniently, Gross' table (<u>Bileam</u>, 422-423). It should be noted that the vast majority of commentators from Wellhausen to the time of Gross' study concur with this allocation.

9. Gross, <u>Bileam</u>, 419-422.

There are, however, serious problems with the source divisions outlined above. As even the staunchest supporters of the documentary hypothesis have noted, the Balaam cycle cannot be parcelled out to J and E on the classic basis of the distribution of the divine names Yahweh and Elohim.[10] We must, therefore, consider other evidence. With specific reference to the ass story, H. Rouillard[11] has convincingly shown that the vocabulary of verses 22-34 shows no particular affinity to either J or E exclusively. Furthermore, if we maintain that 22:2-21 is a blending of J and E, an additional problem is created. Verses 2-21 present a picture of Balaam that paints him as a model Yahweh worshipper.[12] When asked by Balaq's messengers to come and curse Israel, Balaam responds by asking them to wait the night so that he can consult Yahweh on the matter (22:8). When God initially tells him not to go to Balaq (v 12), Balaam promptly informs the emissaries that he is unable to go because Yahweh has refused him permission (v 13). And it is only at God's express command, when the messengers come to him a second time, that Balaam agrees to accompany them (vv 20-21). Yet if both J and E agree that Balaam's behavior is exemplary, as verses 2-21 would have us believe, how could J be responsible for a tradition that not only interrupts the telling of its own story, but also casts

----

10. See, for instance, Albright ("Oracles," 207) and Gray (<u>Numbers</u>, 311).

11. "L'ânesse de Balaam," <u>RB</u> 87 (1980) 26-35.

12. George Coats ("Balaam: Sinner or Saint?," <u>Bib. Research</u> 18 [1973] 21-29) characterizes the Balaam of chapters 22-24, with the exception of 22:22-34, as a legendary saint. By "saint" Coats means a hero whose life exemplifies a significant virtue ("The Way of Obedience: Traditio-Historical and Hermeneutical Reflections on the Balaam Story," <u>Semeia</u> 24 [1982] 56).

Balaam in a downright contradictory light?

Alan Jenks[13] has sought to solve this problem by assigning verses 3-21 and 36-40 exclusively to E, and accounts for inconsistencies within these verses through the growth of tradition in E circles rather than by recourse to J interpolations. He attributes the alternation of divine names within these verses to theological problems created by the case of a foreign seer calling on Yahweh, and stresses that the mode of revelation in verses 3-21 is the night dream, a mode elsewhere in the Tetrateuch characteristic of E.[14] With regard to the argument from theology, Jenk's case would be far more convincing if the text avoided placing Yahweh's name on Balaam's lips, yet stressed that it was indeed Yahweh (and not the generic "god") who in fact dictated Balaam's actions. This, however, is not the case. Invariably the MT has Balaam invoke Yahweh, yet it is the more vague Elohim who tells Balaam what to do. With regard to the latter point, Jenk's argument from the vehicle of revelation (i.e. the night dream) loses force in light of Deir ʿAllā, which clearly depicts Balaam as having visions of deity at night (wyʾtw.ʾlwh ʾlhn.blylh.wyḥz.mḥzh, combination 1.1). Thus the mode of revelation described in verses 3-21 cannot be used as an argument for an exclusively E source because Deir ʿAllā, a tradition presumably independent of E, also records that Balaam received his information through the medium of night visions.

How, then, should we resolve this problem? I

----

13. The Elohist and North Israelite Traditions (Missoula: Scholars, 1977) 57.

14. Jenks, Elohist, 56.

propose the following solution. Although we cannot with assurance disentangle J from E in the Balaam cycle, I think we can maintain, against, for instance, Gross,[15] that the Balaam cycle was a part of the epic tradition[16] evidenced elsewhere in the Tetrateuch.[17] If we posit, then, that the earliest epic tradition(s) about Balaam viewed him positively, the episode of Balaam and the ass, which overtly ridicules Balaam, is best relegated to a later level of tradition. In order to appreciate just how thoroughly Balaam is being mocked in Num 22:22-35 it is instructive to view this passage in light of the finds made at Deir ᶜAllā. It had often been observed prior to the discoveries at Deir ᶜAllā that the fact that Balaam's ass sees the divine messenger while Balaam himself remained unaware of the danger is clearly intended to

----

15. Bileam, passim.

16. For the use of the term "epic tradition" to describe J and E, see F. M. Cross ("The Epic Traditions of Early Israel: Epic Narrative and the Reconstruction of Early Israelite Institutions," R. E. Friedman (ed.), The Poet and the Historian [HSM 26; Chico: Scholars, 1983] 14-19).

17. The most attractive argument for this, in my opinion, has been offered very recently by Brian Peckham (The Composition of the Deuteronomistic History [HSM 35; Atlanta: Scholars, 1985] 5). Peckham notes that J epic tradition begins in the garden of Eden, located at the confluence of the world rivers. The focal point of J, according to Peckham, is the gradual differentiation of the people Israel from the surrounding nations (Composition, 78 n. 25). Thus the chosen people are progressively more closely defined, until we finally arrive at the group Yahweh brought out of Egypt. It is this narrowed people whom Balaam blesses, bringing to a close J's narrative "...as it began with Israel described as a garden free of enchantment (Num 23:23; 24:1) that Yahweh God planted by the water (Num 24:5-6)." (Composition, 5). In the most primitive source of the Tetrateuch, then, Balaam was a wholly positive character who pronounced the final blessing on the people Israel.

ridicule the foreign seer.[18] However, the fact that the ass could see what the seer could not was typically construed as evidence that Balaam was modelled on a Mesopotamian *bārû*.[19] Deir ʿAllā both proves that Balaam need not be construed as a Mesopotamian diviner as well as brings into sharper focus the satirical bent of Num 22:22-35. As was first suggested by P. Kyle McCarter[20] and accepted by Jo Ann Hackett,[21] the abnormal behavior of animals is a central feature of the Balaam tradition preserved in Deir ʿAllā combination 1 (lines 7-11 and perhaps 15-16). Balaam is the one who reports this atypical behavior to his people, in the context of transmitting the gods' intentions to precipitate a cosmic cataclysm. Yet the Balaam of Num 22:22-35 does not perceive that the unusual behavior of his own she-ass bodes personal calamity for him. Balaam's ass actually has to demonstrate to her uncomprehending master that *her* behavior is highly atypical (v 30): "And the ass said to Balaam, 'Am I not your ass upon which you have ridden since time immemorial? Has it indeed been my habit to act this way toward you?'" Far from the seer who perceives a cosmic debacle based on the atypical behavior of animals, this Balaam cannot even perceive the implications in his own life of an animal well-known to him acting in a thoroughly antithetical fashion.

----

18. For example, Rudolph, *Elohist*, 110; Gross, *Bileam*, 359.

19. For example, Albright, "Oracles," 231 n. 141; de Vaulx, *Les Nombres*, 269.

20. "The Balaam Texts from Deir ʿAllā: The First Combination," *BASOR* 239 (1980) 58.

21. *Balaam*, 29.

The Balaam tradition at Deir ʿAllā is not the only tradition from which Num 22:22-35 draws for its telling of the ass story; it also appears to be working with information found in the biblical oracles, specifically Num 24:4b and 16b. These passages speak of a seer who, falling down, has had his eyes uncovered (nōpēl ûgĕlûy ʿênāyim).[22] The ass story clearly describes a man initially blind to the divine presence[23] who sees the celestial messenger only after his ass has collapsed underneath him (22:27). The story of the ass again incorporates information already known about Balaam, and again uses that information to confirm an unflattering portrait of him. It fleshes out, in a satirical fashion, the precise circumstances in which Balaam fell down and had his eyes uncovered.[24]

----

22. The phrase šĕtum hāʿāyin (Num 24:3, 15), rendered by the RSV as "[whose] eye is opened," has been treated by W. F. Albright ("The Oracles of Balaam," JBL 63 [1944] 216-217), who argued that the original text read še-tammá ʿênô, "whose eye is perfect."

23. Rouillard ("L'ânesse," 11) also notes that the ass story shares the theme of opened eyes with Numbers 24.

24. This fleshing out of epic tradition in a derogatory manner would have a further effect, i.e. the details of the ass story relevant to 24:3b-4 and 15b-16 could then be read back into these passages, thus coloring the earlier tradition and effecting a very different understanding of it. Although not directed specifically at the story of Balaam's ass, Geza Vermes' comments (Scripture and Tradition in Judaism: Haggadic Studies [Leiden: Brill, 1973] 176) on this point are extremely appropriate: "The various currents of biblical tradition, whether oral or written, did not remain separate units. A new tradition, whatever its original purpose, neither simply supplemented, nor wholly replaced previous traditions, but through a process of vital osmosis, completely transformed them. By the addition and assimilation of the P account, the Balaam of pre-priestly tradition became a different person."

As I have mentioned above, there is good reason to believe that the earliest tradition about Balaam viewed him not only positively, but even as a critical actor in the progressively narrowing definition of the people of Yahweh's covenant.[25] If we allow that this tradition stems from J, then it is difficult to suppose that J is also responsible for the derisive story of Balaam and the ass. The other epic siglum available to us is E, but in the entire history of modern scholarship, only one scholar has assigned Num 22:22-34 to E.[26] That scholar, C. Steuernagel, in fact assigned the entire Balaam cycle (excluding minor redactional activity) to the E source, thus ignoring the vast disparity in caricature between the Balaam of 22:22-34 and the Balaam of the remainder of the cycle. For this reason, his source assignment cannot be taken seriously. Furthermore, as we have seen above, there is no lexical evidence for assigning 22:22-34 to E. Thus E, too, is an

----

25. In the P organization of epic tradition, Balaam's blessing is set in the plains of Moab, the last station before crossing the Jordan and entering into P's conception of the promised land. Thus the P tradent preserved the traditional connection between Balaam and the people's final "constitutional" blessing, although the tradent no doubt had to move the scene of this blessing in order to bring it into a strictly western Jordanian vision of the land of promise. For textual evidence that the earliest Balaam traditions were not set in the plains of Moab, at P's last station before the entry into Canaan, see Rudolph (Elohist, 101-103). The epic narrative itself associates Balaam with Baamoth-Baal (22:41) Pisgah (23:14) and (Baal) Peor (23:28), and so it is logical to conclude that one or all of these sites were, at an early stage of tradition, considered to be the pivotal point(s) of a Yahwistic confederation of tribes.

26. In 1899, C. Steuernagel proposed assigning it to E^2, and in 1912 revised his opinion to suggest E^s (Gross, Bileam, 422-423).

inappropriate source for the ass story.

If the ass story does not belong to epic tradition, how should we date it and to which source should we assign it? Let us first examine the biblical evidence. Outside Numbers 22-24,[27] the earliest mention of Balaam is a terse reference in Micah 6:5a, which can be dated roughly 740-690 B.C.E.: "O my people, remember what Balaq king of Moab counselled, and how Balaam son of Beor answered him." If we read this excerpt solely in light of epic tradition, there is no hint that Micah viewed Balaam negatively; Balaq proposed to have Balaam curse Israel, and Balaam refused.[28]

The next two passages outside Numbers 22-24 that mention Balaam are Josh 24:9-10 and Deut 23:5-6. Because of certain similarities in vocabulary used in these two passages (see below), I will consider them together.

> And Balaq ben Sippor king of Moab arose and made war on Israel. And he sent and summoned Balaam ben Beor to curse you. But I would not listen to Balaam. Indeed I blessed you and rescued you from his hand.

> An Ammonite or a Moabite shall not enter into the congregation of the Lord, unto the tenth generation none of them shall enter into the congregation of the Lord forever, because they did not meet you with food and water on the journey when you went out of Egypt and because he hired against you Balaam son of Beor from Pethor, Aram-Naharaim, to curse you.

----

27. For discussions of the history of the Balaam tradition, see Rouillard ("L'ânesse," 231-239), Noth (<u>Numbers</u>, 173), Ludwig Schmidt ("Die alttestamentliche Bileamüberlieferung," <u>BZ</u> 23 [1979] 258-260), and J. de Vaulx (<u>Les Nombres</u> [Paris: Gabalda, 1972] 256-263).

28. Cf. Noth, <u>Numbers</u>, 173.

> But Yahweh wouldn't listen to Balaam, and Yahweh your God turned for you the curse into a blessing, for the Lord your God loves you.

Both Josh 24:2-28 and Deut 23:1-9 contain pre-Deuteronomistic materials, stemming in the former passage from league traditions at Shechem[29] and in the latter from Deuteronomic legislation.[30] The tradition about Balaam presented in Deut 23:5-6 has been widely identified as an expansion on the Deuteronomic prohibition against Moabites belonging to the congregation of the Lord.[31] A. D. H. Mayes has proposed that these verses may have been added by a "deuteronomic legislator," a pre-Deuteronomistic hand responsible for formulating much of the material contained in the deuteronomic legal corpus.[32] If, however, we note the phrasing of Deut 23:6a and compare it to Josh 24:10a, we can observe that it is very similar (Deut 23:6a; *wĕlōʾ-ʾābâ yhwh ʾĕlōhêkā lišmōaʿ-ʾel bilʿām*; Josh 24:10a: *wĕlōʾ ʾābîtî lišmōaʿ lĕbilʿām*). The use of the verb *ʾābâ* plus *lāmed* plus infinitive construct occurs frequently throughout the Deuteronomistic history and in passages from the Chronicler's history that are dependent on the Deuteronomistic history; when the subject is Yahweh, the construction is found only in these two places. There is

----

29. F. M. Cross, *Canaanite Myth and Hebrew Epic* (Cambridge: Harvard University, 1973) 85, 133; Boling, *Joshua*, 335.

30. A. D. H. Mayes, *Deuteronomy* (CB; London: Oliphants, 1979) 314-317; Kurt Galling, "Das Gemeindegesetz in Deuteronomium 23," *Festschrift für A. Bertholet*, 1950, 176-191.

31. For example, Mayes, *Deuteronomy*, 316; G. von Rad, *Deuteronomy* (OTL; Philadelphia: Westminster, 1966) 145.

32. Mayes, *Deuteronomy*, 47-48, 52.

good reason to believe, then, that the construction is typical of Dtr^{1},[33] and is one of the expressions used by Dtr^{1} to convey the conviction that Yahweh was in firm control of Israel's history. It seems likely, then, that the traditions about Balaam preserved in Josh 24 and Deut 23 express the viewpoint of Dtr^{1}.

Again, if the above verses concerning Balaam are read solely in the light of epic tradition, they are not overtly hostile; epic tradition knows that Balaq petitioned Balaam to curse Israel (Num 22:6), that Balaam transmitted the request to Yahweh (22:10-11), and that Yahweh refused to cooperate (22:12), and eventually instructed Balaam to speak only as directed (22:20). The main difference between the brief notices about Balaam and Balaq found in Deut 23 and Josh 24 and the story told in the epic tradition of Num 22-24 is the focus of the tellings. In Num 22-24 epic tradition casts Balaam in the starring role, which is to say it focuses on depicting him as an exemplary vehicle of God's will. Balaam will do only as Yahweh instructs him (22:13, 20-21, 38; 23:12, etc.); indeed, in spite of all the treasures that Balaq might offer, Balaam will heed only Yahweh's command (22:18; 24:13). The focus in the Deuteronomistic passages is not Balaam, but Yahweh. Dtr^{1} is stressing Yahweh's role in the episode, which was to turn a potential curse into a blessing.[34] The spotlight has been turned on Yahweh, and the deity's role as

----

33. If it was Dtr^{2} we would not expect it to be present in Chronicles, as the Chronicler worked from an edition of the Deuteronomistic history that had not been reworked by Dtr^{2}. Cf. Steven McKenzie *The Chronicler's Use of the Deuteronomistic History* (HSM 33; Atlanta: Scholars, 1985).

34. Cf. Rouillard, "L'ânesse," 235.

protector of Israel is being stressed. It may be noted, however, that although Dtr^{1}'s comments are not manifestly negative toward Balaam, the shift of stress from Balaam to Yahweh creates the potential for construing Balaam as an inimical character.

For the P redactor, Balaam is clearly a nefarious individual. P credits Balaam (Num 31:16) with prompting the Midianite women to lure the sons of Israel into apostasy at Peor (Num 25:6-18),[35] and further notes that Balaam was killed in a campaign against Midian (Num 31:7-8). The tradition that the Israelites purposely slew Balaam was also known to Dtr^{2} (Josh 13:22)[36] and may be construed as evidence that Dtr^{2}, like P, viewed Balaam negatively.[37] Finally, Neh 13:2 refers to Balaam in the context of citing Deut 23:5-6 as evidence that persons of foreign decent should be excluded from membership in the Israelite covenant community.

To summarize our review of biblical Balaam traditions outside the Balaam cycle, the available evidence suggests that the potential to view Balaam negatively may be latent in the references made to him by Dtr^{1}, although the first clear-cut evidence comes from the exilic period (P, Dtr^{2}). This analysis meshes well with recent scholarly discussion of the date and source of Num 22:22-34, and it is to this topic that I shall now turn.

----

35. Cf. Cross, *Canaanite Myth*, 311, 316.

36. Boling, *Joshua*, 335.

37. Note also that Dtr^{2} calls Balaam a diviner (*qôsēm*). Divination was an activity proscribed by Deuteronomic legislation (Deut 18:10).

Subsequent to Wellhausen and prior to Walter Gross' exhaustive 1974 study of the Balaam cycle,[38] Num 22:22-34 uniformly had been assigned to epic tradition. We have seen above why this must be abandoned. Epic tradition looks approvingly on Balaam, whereas Num 22:22-34 overtly ridicules him. More recently, however, the tide of scholarly opinion has changed toward assigning the ass story to a later stratum of tradition. Gross, for instance, attributes the ass story to the latest of the four sources that he finds in the Balaam cycle.[39] H. Rouillard sees close similarities between the tone of Num 22:22-34 and that of Deut 23:5-6;[40] she dates the ass story on thematic grounds ca. 600-550 B.C.E..[41] Alexander Rofé[42] assigns Num 22:22-34 to the latest redaction of the Balaam cycle, which he dates to the 6th-5th centuries B.C.E.. Brian Peckham[43] identifies the ass story on the grounds of redactional technique as an insertion of Dtr^2, which in his schema is the final redactional strand of the collected books of Genesis through 2 Kings. In short, whereas these scholars do not agree precisely on the chronological particulars of their respective source analyses, all date the ass story to the 6th century B.C.E. or later, and three of them assign it

----

38. Gross, Bileam.

39. Gross, Bileam, 364-369.

40. Rouillard, "L'ânesse," 234.

41. Rouillard, "L'ânesse," 231, 238.

42. The Book of Balaam (Jerusalem: Sinor, 1979) [Hebrew]. Cited by Y. Gitay in a book review, JBL 100 (1981) 471.

43. Composition, figure 7.

specifically to the level that each identifies as the latest level of redactional activity.[44] For the purposes of this study it is not critical to decide amongst the precise options that have been proposed. What is important is that all indicators point toward abandoning the position that Num 22:22-34 stems from epic tradition, and recognizing instead that it is the product of a much later hand.

----

44. My own inclination would be to assign the ass story to P. That P's hand can be discerned elsewhere in Numbers 22 is made most obvious by the inclusion of the Midianites in Balaq's plan to curse Israel (22:4, 7). Their role in the procurement of Balaam is shadowy, unessential, and inconsistent, and their presence in Numbers 22 has often been identified by modern scholarship as the work of a redactional hand. (For example, J. E. Carpenter and G. H. Battersby, *The Hexateuch* [New York: Longman's, Green and Co., 1900] 225; Gray, *Numbers*, 323; Noth, *Numbers*, 176.) Given both the clearly P tradition associating Balaam with the Midianites (Num 31:8, 16) and P's general antipathy toward Midian (see F. M. Cross, *Canaanite Myth*, 311, 316), it is reasonable to suspect that P was also responsible for writing the Midianites into Numbers 22. Their addition at this point serves to prepare the reader for the following episode, the apostasy at Baal Peor (Num 25), which ties illicit cult practices involving Moabite women in the epic source (vv 1-5) to P's assertion that the Midianites were also implicated in the event (vv 6-18; Cross, *Canaanite Myth*, 316). The Midianites' inclusion in chapter 22, then, brings the Midianites onto the scene and places them in collusion with the Moabites, thus "explaining" how, in chapter 25, both Moabites and Midianites were present, united by the goal of bringing Israel to harm. If P was responsible for introducing the Midianites into chapters 22 and 25 because of its general antipathy toward Midian, and if we know that P not only had a highly unfavorable opinion of Balaam but also that P is the only tradition that specifically links Balaam with the Midianites at Peor, it is reasonable to suspect that P might also have introduced into the Balaam cycle a tradition that cast the foreign seer in an unfavorable light. The case, however, is not airtight, and thus attribution of the ass story to P must remain a suspicion.

I have dealt at length with the questions of dating and source attribution because the resolution of these questions has a tremendous impact on one's overall conceptualization of how the term <u>śāṭān</u> is used in the Hebrew Bible when referring to the divine sphere. First of all, Kluger's evolutionary model of a developing Satan concept must be viewed with extreme caution if not entirely abandoned. Because she dates the ass story significantly earlier than Job 1-2, Zechariah 3 and 1 Chronicles 21, Kluger identifies Numbers 22 as the locus in which the profane "Satan concept" was transposed into the mythical sphere.[45] That Yahweh could act as a <u>śāṭān</u>[46] is for Kluger the first stage.[47] This same function was later transferred to one of the <u>bĕnê ʾĕlōhîm</u> (Job 1-2, Zech 3) and given the status of a mythological personality.[48] Later still (1 Chr 21) the term <u>śāṭān</u> was divorced from the divine council context and became the proper name of an independent personality.[49]

As I shall demonstrate in the chapter dealing with <u>śāṭān</u> in 1 Chronicles 21, the term in that passage is not used as a proper name. If there is no Satan in 1 Chronicles 21 then there is no Satan in the Hebrew Bible, hence to talk about a profane Satan concept is, within the context of the Hebrew Bible texts that use the term

----

45. Kluger, <u>Satan</u>, 29, 31, 57.

46. Kluger (<u>Satan</u>, 68-69) views the <u>malʾāk yhwh</u> as an "exterior soul," and hence states that the real <u>śāṭān</u> of Numbers 22 is Yahweh (<u>Satan</u>, 75). In that the function of the messenger is to do the master's will, I would agree.

47. Kluger, <u>Satan</u>, 64, 76.

48. Kluger, <u>Satan</u>, 39.

49. Kluger, <u>Satan</u>, 155.

śāṭān, anachronistic. In heaven as on earth, the term *śāṭān* had neither a single meaning nor a sole referent. And when Satan as it were materializes as an independent personality the traits attributed to him definitely include reflections of and implications drawn from certain of the texts that employ the noun *śāṭān*, but what we might call Satan's fundamental purpose and nature was not derived from *any* of the biblical *śāṭān* texts. Without the fundamental notion of a semi-autonomous archfiend who wields the forces of evil against God's will and to the detriment of all humankind, there is no Satan. As many before me have said, this notion seems not to have been an organic product of home-grown Israelite speculation, but rather was borrowed from Zoroastrianism and grafted onto certain branches of early Judaic thought. If this was indeed the case, then to speak of the development of a concept *prior to its introduction* is ludicrous. The notion may be said to have evolved on its own soil and within its own thoughtworld, and may be said to evolve in Judeo-Christian thought after its introduction, but it cannot be said to have developed in Israel prior to the time that it was introduced into the biblical stream of consciousness.

Because Kluger attributes Num 22:22-34 to early (=epic) tradition, she draws the conclusion that Yahweh functioned as a *śāṭān* only in the most archaic level of narrative tradition. Once we recognize, however, that that the ass story derives not from the tenth century J source but rather from the sixth century B.C.E. or later, the chronological basis upon which Kluger's model rests collapses. The ass story may still be earlier than the other three passages that mention a celestial *śāṭān*, but only marginally so, and depending on how one dates

Job 1-2, the ass story may even postdate the Joban prologue. Furthermore, whereas the sword-wielding messenger of Numbers 22 is the only instance of the mal'āk yhwh specifically designated as a śāṭān, 2 Samuel 24//1 Chronicles 21 describes the mal'āk yhwh, sword in hand, likewise dispatched by Yahweh to carry out the divine will. Given the similarity of description and the functional equivalence it seems reasonable to conclude that although the text does not explicitly say so, the sword-wielding messenger of 2 Samuel 24//1 Chronicles 21 has also been dispatched lĕśāṭān.[50]

Kluger also remarks that śāṭān as used in Numbers 22 is a functional concept and not a mythological figure.[51] Whereas she does not use this as excuse to dismiss treating Numbers 22 along with Job, Zechariah and Chronicles, it is a fact that Numbers 22 has very often been ignored by scholars who have discussed the term śāṭān[52] even though the term is specifically applied to a divine being. I think that Kluger is right to make some kind of qualitative distinction between śāṭān as used in Numbers 22 and the way it is used in Job and Zechariah, and in that the mal'āk yhwh is neither an evil spirit nor, like Satan, God's opponent, it is

----

50. The same could be said, I think, of the enigmatic mašḥît (Exod 12:23) dispatched to kill the first-born of Egypt.

51. Kluger, Satan, 39.

52. For example, Numbers 22 is not treated by Duhm (Die bösen Geister), Kaupel (Die Dämonen), Lods ("Les origines") or Gaster ("Satan"). Brock-Unte ("Der Fiend") mentions Numbers 22, but it is one of the passages that does not fit his reconstruction of the social context that generated the term śāṭān.

understandable that scholars interested in those phenomena do not discuss Numbers 22. But if the ass story is not J, and therefore does not significantly predate Job, Zechariah and Chronicles, then we should not explain that distinction between function and figure as a movement or development, but rather must account for the difference in some other way.

As was pointed out in the introduction, śāṭān means both "adversary" in general and "legal opponent" in particular. Even if we grant that śāṭān as used in Job and Zechariah may point toward the institutionalization of a legal-adversarial role in the divine council, this does not mean that śāṭān in its more general sense was simultaneously either restricted or abandoned, or that the legal-adversarial role was confined to that office. The respective uses of the term need not be put on a time line; various meanings could well have existed side by side, as indeed the Akkadian term bēl dabābi meant both adversary and legal opponent in contemporaneous texts.

The final topic that I shall discuss is the malʾāk yhwh's statement to Balaam about the reason why he has been dispatched to impede Balaam's journey. In verse 32, after Yahweh has uncovered Balaam's eyes so that he can see the divine messenger, the malʾāk speaks as follows: hinnēh ʾānōkî yāṣāʾtî lĕśāṭān kî yāraṭ hadderek lĕnegdî. The first half of this statement is clear; the messenger is asserting that he has come forth as a śāṭān. The second part contains a crux, the verb yāraṭ, which was a problem even for the ancient translators of the biblical text.[53] Modern scholars translate yāraṭ by

----

53. For collection and discussion of the various ways the phrase was translated in antiquity, see Rouillard ("L'ânesse," 218-219, n. 4) and Gross (Bileam, 165-168).

recourse to Arabic wariṭa and comparison with Job 16:11b, the latter being the only other place in the Hebrew Bible where the root yrṭ is attested.[54] The meaning arrived at is "be precipitate, rush, be hasty."[55] Seeing as it is singularly difficult to understand how a road could be described as hasty, hadderek is best translated as "journey." In addition to "before me" in the physical sense, lĕnegdî can also mean "before me" in the sense of "in my evaluation" or "in my judgment."[56] The entire sentence then reads, "I have come forth as a śāṭān because the journey was hasty in my judgment." What this means, quite obviously, is that Balaam set out on his journey without consulting Yahweh.[57] Thus verse 32 refers back to verse 22, where we were told that God became angry on account of Balaam's going (wayyiḥar-ʾap ʾĕlōhîm kî hôlēk hûʾ). The reader already knows why the messenger has been dispatched--because God was angry about Balaam's departure--but Balaam did not know the cause of divine wrath. In verse 32, the messenger tells him why. If this interpretation is correct, it is no wonder that the ancient translators did not arrive at the same conclusion. The ancients would have understood this verse in light of the broader context of chapter 22, which states that Balaam consulted with Yahweh twice.

----

54. In fact, Job 16:11 is pointed as if the root were rṭh, but virtually all Job scholars understand the root to be yrṭ. (See the standard commentaries.)

55. Cf. BDB 437b.

56. Cf. BDB 617b.

57. For the consultation of deity before setting out on a journey, see Judg 18:5. When Yahweh approves of a journey, he sends his messenger hiṣlîaḥ hadderek, literally "to make the journey prosperous" (Gen 24:40). Numbers 22 demonstrates what can happen if Yahweh does not approve.

Once we fully recognize how different the tone and intent of Num 22:22-34 is from the rest of the Balaam cycle and therefore separate it from its immediate context, we are able to recover the meaning of the *malʾāk yhwh*'s message.

If we allow that the announcement of divine wrath is a paralegal expression,[58] then Balaam in verse 32 stands charged with undertaking a journey without divine consent. In verse 34 Balaam acknowledges his guilt by uttering the stock legal confession *ḥāṭāʾtî*,[59] and offers to right the wrong by turning back. The messenger allows him to continue his journey on the condition that he speak only as instructed, which condition is a further proof that the ass story is predicated upon the assumption that Balaam undertook his journey without first consulting Yahweh.

----

58. McCarthy, "Wrath," 100.

59. Boecker, *Redeformen*, 111-114.

Chapter 5

THE *śāṭān* IN THE BOOK OF JOB

But in the book of Job, Milton's Messiah is call'd Satan.
- William Blake, *The Marriage of Heaven and Hell.*

You realize by now the part you played
To stultify the Deuteronomist
And change the tenor of religious thought.
My thanks are to you for releasing me
From moral bondage to the human race.
- God, addressing Job, in Robert Frost's *A Masque of reason*.

The book of Job is, in many ways, the most challenging book of the Hebrew Bible. From those trained in Hebrew its grammar and diction command as a response both awe and humility, a reaction consistent, perhaps intentionally consistent, with the book's portrayal of Job's response to revealed deity.[1] On the compositional level it defies neat categorization, bursting the bounds of any genre thus far proposed to contain it. And on the level of message, the widely and wildly divergent interpretations offered throughout the ages bespeak its tangled complexity.

There is no "correct" reading of the book of Job. It sets up a hypothetical situation which it asks the reader (or, more primitively, the listener) to contemplate: a man *tām wĕyāšār*, a man of exemplary integrity, is made to suffer. In what follows I will be

----

1. Contra John Briggs Curtis, "On Job's Response to Yahweh," *JBL* 98 (1979) 497-511. Curtis sees in Job's response (40:4-5, 42:2-6) a rejection of transcendent deity (p. 510).

arguing that the story is told in such a way that, initially at least, it need not be regarded as factual in the same way as the Deuteronomistic history, for instance, portrays David's dealings with the ousted house of Saul. In the latter example, propaganda is presented as historical fact; in the book of Job we are presented, initially, with a folktale. In the Deuteronomistic history, it is clear what we are being asked to believe; in the book of Job, there is room for discussion, and more important, individual reaction. The book of Job seeks to inspire thought, to endorse complexity, ambiguity, and paradox. It actively challenges the reader or listener to contemplate its contents and debate its meaning, and because of this very dialogue between the work itself and its audience[2] it is in the final analysis multivalent.

Having granted that the reader or listener, both modern and in antiquity, has a certain amount of interpretational autonomy when approaching the book of Job, I would like to distinguish between the modern reader and his or her ancient counterpart. A book is read or a story heard against the backdrop of cultural and political context, and thus resonates differently for different audiences. In what follows, I hope to reappropriate something of the social and theological context against which the book of Job was primitively heard. In preparation for this and other tasks, I shall first discuss the compositional integrity of the Masoretic book of Job.

The book of Job can be broadly divided into

----

2. Cf. Edwin M. Good, "Job and the Literary Task: A Response," Soundings 56 (1973) 472-473.

prologue, dialogue cycle, wisdom poem, Elihu speeches, whirlwind speeches, and epilogue.[3] Given both the mixture of genres and perceived inconsistencies amongst the various sections of the book, early scholarship viewed Job as something of a cut-and-paste job none too carefully executed.[4] The whirlwind speeches, often claimed to be irrelevant because they do not address Job's demand for an explanation of his suffering, were, and remain, a particularly vexing problem.[5] In theory I suppose it is possible that the main sections of the book do not really fit together, but if the theory is pursued to its logical conclusion, the book of Job in its present form has, and had, no meaning. If the juxtaposition of its parts was haphazard, message is eradicated. Thus it seems more profitable to posit a basic integrity to the book of Job, and try to make sense of the component parts in light of the overall composition.

Indeed, the most recent studies[6] of the book of Job affirm its basic structural integrity. For the purposes of this study, I will focus on the broad relationship between the prose prologue and epilogue and the poetic dialogues, and comment only briefly on the

----

3. See, for example, Marvin Pope (Job [AB 15; Garden City: Doubleday, 1965] xxiii-xxx) and Yair Hoffman ("The Relation Between the Prologue and the Speech Cycles in Job," VT 31 [1981] 162).

4. E.g. B. Duhm, Das Buch Job (Tübingen, 1897) viii, 10-11.

5. I will be addressing this problem below.

6. For a convenient review of scholarship from 1954 to 1981, see Ronald J. Williams ("Current Trends in the Study of the Book of Job," Walter Aufrecht [ed.], Studies in the Book of Job [Waterloo: Wilfred Laurier, 1985] 1-27).

whirlwind speeches. Although the folktale told in the prologue and epilogue,[7] for instance, may have had in some form of its telling[8] a life independent of the material now spliced into its middle, there is ample evidence to suggest that it has been retold, reshaped, in conscious appreciation of the poetic section of the work.[9] Norman Habel has described this evidence as "signals of continuity" between the prose and poetic

----

7. The story told in the prose prologue and epilogue is commonly refered to as a folktale. See William Whedbee ("The Comedy of Job," Semeia 7 [1977] 5-6) and David Robertson ("The Book of Job: A Literary Study," Soundings 56 [1973] 447) for discussion of the folktale form. To excerpt from Whedbee ("Comedy," 5), "It has the customary 'once upon a time' fairy tale beginning: 'There was a man in the land of Uz, whose name was Job' (1:1). The setting in a non-Israelite locale, the vaguely defined land of Uz, heightens this dimension. The stylized numbers--seven sons and three daughters, seven thousand sheep and three thousand oxen--contribute further to the folktale flavor, as does the adroit use of repetition (a twofold test, a four-fold series of disasters each of which is laconically reported by an anonymous messenger, a twofold audience between Yahweh and the Satan). Moreover, the characters are stylized, being defined by formulas and motifs typical of folktales. So Job is the best of men, 'the greatest of all the peoples of the east' (1:3b). He always does the right thing at the right time--whether in prosperity or adversity." Cf. Ezek 14:14, 20.

8. The folktale, by definition, would have existed in multiform.

9. This statement affirms both the work of Nahum Sarna ("Epic Substratum in the Book of Job," JBL 76 [1957] 13-25) and that of Avi Hurvitz ("The Date of the Prose-Tale of Job Linguistically Reconsidered," HTR 67 [1974] 17-34) in that it grants the folktale deep traditional roots, but asserts that the telling found in the book of Job does not strictly reproduce, on the level of grammar and diction, what might be expected in earlier tellings.

sections of the book.[10] For example, we can compare 1:10, a verse found in the prologue, with 3:23, a verse located in Job's opening dialogue speech. In chapter one, the *śāṭān* claims that Job worships God because God ensures his material well-being by encircling Job with a protective hedge.[11] It is only when Yahweh agrees to remove that protective hedge and allows the *śāṭān* to touch Job's family and possessions that Job is plunged into suffering. Yet in chapter three, Job attributes his *suffering* to the fact that God hedges him round about![12] Thus we are presented with a contradiction; should we then view the prologue and dialogue as ill fitted compositional units? Habel argues, and I agree, that we should not.[13] The interplay between various terms and motifs shared by the narrative and poetic sections of the book are often better understood as conscious dramatic irony than unplanned contradiction and inconsistency.[14]

----

10. Norman Habel, "The Narrative Art of Job," *JSOT* 27 (1983) 102-104. Cf. Habel, *The Book of Job* (OTL; Philadelphia: Westminster Press, 1985) 25-31; Rick Moore, "The Integrity of the Book of Job," *CBQ* 42 (1983) 17-31; Hoffman, "Prologue and Speech Cycles," 160-170.

11. "The *śāṭān* answered Yahweh and said, 'Is it for nothing that Job fears God? Don't you hedge in [*śaktā*] him, his household, and everything that belongs to him?'" (1:9-10a).

12. *wayyāsek ʾĕlôah baʿădô*.

13. Habel, *Job*, 24, 52.

14. Habel, "Narrative Art," 104. On this general point, cf. Whedbee ("Comedy," 1-39), Robertson ("Job," 446-449), James G. Williams (" 'You have not spoken truth of me': Mystery and Irony in Job," *ZAW* 83 [1971] 231-255), William Power ("A Study of Irony in the Book of Job," Ph.D. dissertation, University of Toronto, 1961) and J. Gerald Janzen (*Job* [Atlanta: John Knox, 1985] 17-18). J. C. Holbert (" 'The Skies Will Uncover His Iniquity': Satire in the Second Speech of Zophar [Job

Job is not privy to the celestial machinations that set into motion his fall from health and prosperity; thus his statement in 3:23 cannot be said to contradict 1:10. Rather, it is a misperception, an ironic misperception, of Job's relationship to his deity. The irony is not apparent to Job because he is ignorant of the scene set in the prologue, but is readily available to the audience who, unlike the characters of the dialogues, are aware of the precise celestial events leading to Job's misfortunes. Recognition of the disparity between what the audience knows and what the characters of the dialogues know, and the possibilities for irony that this disparity creates, are tremendously important factors in this chapter's understanding of the śāṭān in the book of Job.

A few preliminary remarks need to be made about the primitive audience of the book of Job. Broadly speaking, the book of Job challenges the traditional assumption of a direct correspondence between a mortal's deeds and his or her material prosperity; that is, it challenges the assumption that the righteous should inevitably prosper. Unless we posit that the book of Job was preaching to the converted, we must assume that the intended audience included persons who believed this axiom to be true. How did the author choose to challenge the traditional assumptions of his audience? William Whedbee has suggested that the book of Job should be read as a comedy, and notes that comedy has often served as a strategy for dealing with chaos and suffering,[15] the same chaos and suffering that the orthodox belief in

----

20]," VT 31 [1981] 171) sees the repeated use of satire, which he defines as "militant irony," in the book of Job.

15. Whedbee, "Comedy," 4.

rightful retribution was designed to address. Whereas I do not deny that comedy can be an effective vehicle for challenging traditional assumptions,[16] I do not think that comedy is the primary means by which the book of Job persuades its audience to contemplate its message. Rather, I think that it is the juxtaposition of fantasy and reality--of folktale world and real world--that persuades the orthodox members of the audience to listen and encourages them to take seriously the book's critique of their position.

Although it has been generally recognized that the prologue is told in the form of a folktale,[17] the

----

16. For example, on the television show "Saturday Night Live," there is a segment in which the week's news is reviewed by one or more of the program's regular comics. The stage is set to resemble a "real" newsroom, but the audience knows that they are about to witness a parody of a serious newscast. The stories of horror and destruction that are presented are dealt with through the medium of comedy. This is not to say that "Saturday Night Live" presents the news without having a moral point to make; very often it does, and the point is typically a caustic one. Indeed, by framing their critique in the comic mode, they are "allowed" to be almost indecently irreverent, to cut extremely close to the moralistic bone, and in fact have a much better chance of stimulating those whose morality they are criticizing than if they attempted to discuss the issues through serious dialogue.

17. E.g. Robert Gordis, _The Book of Job_ (New York: Jewish Theological Seminary, 1978) 2; Samuel Terrien, _Job: Poet of Existence_ (New York: Bobbs-Merrill, 1957) 30; Pope, _Job_, xxiv. Earlier scholarship, although not always employing the term "folktale," did recognize the "ideal," "artificial," (Edward Kissane, _The Book of Job_ [New York: Sheed and Ward, 1946] xiv) or "once upon a time" (S. R. Driver and G. B. Gray, _The Book of Job_, vol. 1 [ICC 14; New York: Scribner's, 1921] 2) quality of the prologue. Jewish tradition also recognized the ahistorical nature of the story of Job by terming Job a _māšāl_, "proverb" (Baba Bathra 14b).

implications of the folktale form have not been fully explored. I suggest that the folktale form serves three purposes: it allows the audience to be sure that Job is not to blame for the calamities that befall him, it allows the *śāṭān* to accuse God[18] of divine patronage,[19] and thereby challenge the traditional perception of world order,[20] and it allows the audience to contemplate this

----

18. That Yahweh himself is the primary target of the *śāṭān*'s accusation was suggested to me by Frank Moore Cross and Paul Mosca.

19. Habel (*Job*, 90-91) broaches this topic when he states that "... the Satan sees Yahweh as the culprit because he has made Job the greatest man on earth." While this observation is correct, I think that the accusation is even more profound. Not only is Job's lot being called into question, but the very validity of a system which rewards the righteous with material prosperity is being challenged. If the righteous inevitably prosper, how do we know that their righteousness is motivated by true piety and not base greed?

20. Douglas A. Knight ("Cosmogony and Order in the Hebrew Tradition," Robin W. Lovin [ed.], *Cosmogony and Ethical Order* [Chicago: University of Chicago Press, 1985] 145) states: "The myth of the act-consequence syndrome [i.e. just retribution]...underscores this sense that the 'good creation' is functional, reliable, and moral at its most basic level... The belief in order is connected directly with the problem of theodicy." Not only does just retribution underscore the good creation, I think it was also conceived, in some sense, as being "built into" world order. In other words, moral order is grounded in the orders of creation, both in primordial time and in ongoing world order. As H. H. Schmid ("Creation, Righteousness, and Salvation," B. W. Anderson [ed.], *Creation in the Old Testament* [Philadelphia: Fortress, 1984] 104-105) has observed, the laws of Hammurapi are preceded by a prologue describing the creation of Babylon, its selection by the gods for pre-eminence, and the legitimation of its kingship. The laws, then, are traced back to or grounded in creation. In the biblical world, the same principle was operative, I think, in attributing to the Mosaic period the vast bulk of Israelite law; the time of Moses preceded the existence of Israel as a discrete geographical and political

charge without forsaking, for the moment at least, their own religious orthodoxy.[21]

The folktale, by definition, is a "once upon a time" story; in other words, it is believed to be fictitious.[22] Entering into the world of the folktale involves a suspension of disbelief, because the world of the folktale need not operate according to the rules of observed reality. The Joban prologue, by employing the folktale form, offers the audience a proposition they need not regard as true: what if the link between piety and reward was to be (temporarily) severed? By framing this proposition in the form of a folktale, the orthodox could both entertain the proposition at a safe distance as well as cling, initially at least, to their belief that in the real world the righteous prosper.

The prologue also makes it possible for the audience to entertain the prospect that a totally blameless person exists without challenging the

----

entity, and the order of that society is grounded in the historicized myth of its creation. Furthermore, moral and natural order share some of the same lexicon. For instance, *mišpāṭ* refers to justice in a legal and moral sense as well as to natural order (cf. Good, "Job," 479-480 for references). Finally, I would point to Prov 8:22-31 which depicts wisdom (including just retribution, vv 18 and 20) as one of the first works of creation, thus clearly integrating moral order and world order (cf. Isa 54:11-17; Ps 19).

21. Cf. Hoffman ("Prologue and Speech Cycles," 168-169), who states that the tale form is well suited to the dogmatic reader as well as the sceptic, because the former are assuaged by knowing that the ending will be a happy one, and the latter are perceptive enough to realize that the literary form is a mask to be discarded.

22. Linda Dégh, "Folk Narrative," Richard M. Dorson (ed.), *Folklore and Folklife* (Chicago: University of Chicago, 1972) 60.

observation that no such person exists in reality.[23] In other words, the dialogues are based on the premise that Job has not sinned and is therefore undeserving of the calamities that overtake him.[24] Without this presupposition, the dialogues lose all force. Because Job is a character in a folktale, and because folktales

----

23. This is not to say that the problem of the righteous sufferer was a theme restricted to folklore; indeed, it was a common ancient Near Eastern wisdom theme. The point I am making is that, within the folktale genre, the premise of a totally blameless person could be accepted, at the outset, even by the most cynical critic of human nature. In fact I think it is precisely the use of the folktale genre in the book of Job that separates Job from his counterparts in compositions such as _The Poem of the Righteous Sufferer_ and _Ludlul bēl nēmeqi_. The audience can _know_ of a certainty that Job is innocent, whereas in spite of the protestations of, for instance, Šubše-mešrê-šakkan in _Ludlul_, in the mind of the reader or listener his innocence cannot be absolutely assured. Therefore in _Ludlul_ Šubše-mešrê-šakkan can state that his condition perplexes him (2.1-22) and can conclude that humankind does not know the mind of the gods (2.36-38), but his innocence _per se_ is not affirmed. In the real world, one can never be sure that one has not committed an inadvertent offense, but in the folktale prologue to Job we _know_ that Job is blameless, and hence the book of Job is able to challenge the doctrine of retribution without being susceptible to objections based on recourse to the inscrutability of the divine. Consequently _Ludlul_ ends up reinforcing a traditional position but the book of Job does not.

24. As Paul Ricoeur (_The Symbolism of Evil_ [Boston: Beacon, 1967] 315 n.1) put it, "There is no need to ask whether such a just man [i.e. Job] existed, nor even whether such a man is possible. Job is the _imaginary_ personage who serves as a touchstone for the ethical vision of the world and makes it fly to pieces. By hypothesis or by construction, Job is innocent; he must be just in order that the problem may be posed in all its intensity: how is it possible that a man so wholly just should be so totally suffering? ...Job is the zero degree of guilt joined to the extreme of suffering; from this conjunction is born the scandal which is also extreme."

need not operate by the rules of observed reality, the audience can accept the premise of a blameless man. If the prologue had been set in the real world, this claim, so central to the ensuing movement of the book, could have been easily challenged.

Two of the primary reasons that folktales are told are to entertain and to instruct. When dealing with the divine sphere, the entertainment value of the folktale can be expressed in its irreverence for sober religious speculation and dogma.[25] This is a make-believe world, and thus its divine as well as its human components need not adhere to the normal rules. It is my contention that the scenes of the divine assembly may also evidence disrespect for traditional speculation about the assembly's workings. The freedom inherent in the folktale form allows the prologue to posit a scene in which a celestial accuser turns on Yahweh, master of the assembly, and challenges the validity of Yahweh's blueprint for divine-human relations.

That Job 1:6-13 and 2:1-7 portray meetings of the divine council is clear. The image of Yahweh surrounded by the celestial court is the traditional setting for council scenes (e.g. 1 Kgs 22:19; Isa 6:2-3; Zech 3:4, 7). Furthermore, two of the cited examples depict the convening of the divine court for the purpose of "fixing the fates." In Isaiah 6, the council convenes to determine the fate of Judah after the death of Uzziah (6:1), and in 1 Kings 22 it is to fix Ahab's fate in a

----

25. For example, Max Lüthi (Once Upon a Time: On the Nature of Fairy Tales [Bloomington: Indiana University, 1976] 115) points out that in German folktales, the devil is often depicted as stupid and plodding, contrary to his image in serious theological speculation.

battle against the Arameans of Ramoth-Gilead. In Job, too, the notion is fostered that the council has gathered with the purpose of determining human fate, specifically the lot of Job (1:8). In the opening verses (1:1-6) the audience has been introduced to Job as a paragon of human piety.[26] The scene then switches to the heavenly assembly, with Yahweh touting Job's outstanding virtues. But instead of acquiescence, Yahweh's testimony is met with an atypical challenge (1:9-11). Yahweh is charged by a celestial accuser with protecting Job, his family, and his possessions (v 10). Of course Job is righteous; it brings him health and prosperity. But the test of true righteousness would be worship without the promise of reward. The *śāṭān* is implicitly challenging Yahweh's blueprint for world order; if the righteous always prosper, how can it be ascertained that their behavior is not motivated by material gain?[27] The *śāṭān* is not accusing Job, or at least not directly. He is attacking the problem at its source, by accusing the creator of perpetrating a perverse world order. David Robertson[28] has suggested that in chapter three the test shifts from a test of Job's loyalty to a trial of God, and Edwin Good[29] has proposed that Yahweh's speeches from the whirlwind shift the issue of the book from morality to

----

26. Note that the audience has been told of his exemplary piety in the first verse, and *then* told what his piety has brought him- seven sons, three daughters, and all manner of wealth. In other words, things are introduced in the "right" order; exemplary piety precedes material wealth.

27. An unpleasant question, and it is no wonder that he was later consigned to hell for asking it.

28. "Job," 451.

29. "Job," 481.

world order. I am suggesting that Yahweh is on trial, for his conduct of world order, from the very beginning.

Once it is recognized that Yahweh is being indicted for his blueprint of world order, it is no longer necessary to characterize the interaction between Yahweh and the accuser as it is often characterized in scholarly literature, i.e. as a wager.[30] Job's sufferings are not initiated by some cruel bet, but rather by a profound questioning of the validity of a moral order in which the righteous unfailingly prosper. When charged with perpetrating such a world order, Yahweh responds by allowing the accuser to sever the link between piety and reward; although Job is blameless, he is made to forfeit family and prosperity, and eventually his own good health. The *śāṭān*'s charge can only be proved false if his contention is tested.

----

30. The most recent example is Habel (*Job*, 527). A notable exception is Edwin Good ("Job," 475), who recognizes that "the wager [in the Joban prologue] is a figment of Western imagination," although he makes this statement for a different reason. Good sees in 1:11 and 2:5 a curse formula that *forces* Yahweh to test Job: "Job's suffering is brought on by the Satan's curse on himself, a curse that must operate inexorably and with no moral strings attached to it." ("Job," 475). Good does not spell out the precise reason why he understands the *śāṭān*'s words as a self-curse, but presumably he is referring to the formulas introduced in 1:11 and 2:5 by *ʾim-lōʾ*. Whereas *ʾim-lōʾ* can indeed function as part of an oath formula (e.g. Num 14:28; Jos 14:9), it need not necessarily do so; instead, it can introduce a forcefully made statement, equivalent to the English "surely" (e.g. 1 Kgs 20:23). The function of *ʾim-lōʾ* in 1:11 and 2:5 is at least ambiguous, although if Good is correct, it is added evidence that the *śāṭān* is issuing a legal charge. Job's final indictment of God in chapter 31 is accompanied by a series of explicit self-curses (vv 5-8, 9-10,16-22,38-40), thus demonstrating a link between self imprecation and indictment.

If we understand the interaction between Yahweh and the *śāṭān* to involve a challenge of world order, both Job's opening dialogue speech (ch. 3) and Yahweh's answer from the whirlwind (chs. 38-41) become more intelligible. By allowing the accuser to visit calamity upon a blameless man, world order is effectively rescinded, thus plunging Job's world into chaos. The dialogues open with Job cursing the day of his birth (3:1), during the course of which, as Michael Fishbane has observed,[31] Job essentially reverses the order of creation and thus symbolically returns the universe to primordial chaos. Thus it can be said that Job, in his initial speech, perceives the implications of his plight; if he, a blameless man, is suffering, then retributive justice and the world order of which it is a part must have collapsed. Yahweh, in the whirlwind speeches, also addresses the issues of creation and world order. In the world of the whirlwind speeches, moral order is conspicuously absent.[32] Yahweh in effect describes a world devoid of retributive justice,[33] which is to say the world that the *śāṭān* insisted upon so that true

----

31. M. Fishbane, "Jeremiah 4:23-26 and Job 3:3-13: A Recovered Use of the Creation Pattern," *VT* 21 (1971) 151-167.

32. As Matitiahu Tsevat (*The Meaning of the Book of Job and Other Bible Studies* [New York: Ktav, 1980] 29) puts it, God, in the whirlwind speeches, leads Job through the macrocosm and the microcosm, but nowhere does he show Job justice. Ricoeur (*Symbolism*, 321) notes that the words addressed to Job from the whirlwind do not answer Job's problem: "they are in no way a reconstruction, at a higher degree of subtlety, of the ethical vision of the world."

33. Good ("Job," 479-480) corroborates this point when he sees in 40:8 that God is asking Job whether "...the order of things has necessarily to do with wickedness or innocence.".

righteousness could be tested. A suffering and impoverished Job bends his knee to the god who created and maintains this amoral world, thus proving the accuser wrong.

Having demonstrated a few of the advantages to construing the interaction between Yahweh and the *śāṭān* as a challenge to world order, I would like to return for a moment to the issue of prologue as folktale and audience reaction. I have stated that the folktale form allows the audience to accept the accuser's challenge to world order without necessarily surrendering the belief that in the "real" world, the world mediated to them by traditional wisdom, righteousness engenders well-being. This, indeed, is the initial situation. But in chapter three, the book of Job leaves the land of fantasy and abruptly enters the real world. The cardboard character of Job all at once becomes animated, and he rails against his misfortune. Herein lies the genius of the book of Job. The audience, comfortable with an amoral universe when it is set in a world of make-believe, suddenly has the proverbial rug pulled out from under them. Although they have not been told that the fairytale façade is about to crumble and real life rise up in its place, the actors all of a sudden take on human dimensions. All at once the audience is viewing a real-life drama, but the laws that define that drama, the parameters established by the folktale, become the "real" explanation for a very human Job's misfortunes. In a subtle and unprepossessing manner, what was once styled as fantasy is now laying claims on reality. And in *this* real world, a blameless man is suffering.

The audience, then, has been led into a real world where traditional wisdom does not work. By founding the world of the dialogues on the proposition of the folktale prologue, the audience has been subtly coerced into leaving their traditional assumptions behind, and entertaining a world that is founded on a radical premise. Traditional wisdom, represented by the three friends, is exposed as flummery.

The book of Job begins its journey in the realm of the folktale, and it is to that realm that it returns in the epilogue. The epilogue has often been viewed as a gratuitous ending, a sorry and farcical resolution to a deep problem. After all that Job has been through, the restoration of his fortune rings hollow, if not absurd. But if we pay attention to form, we once again can perceive genius at work. The book of Job ends where it began, in the land of fantasy, but there is a significant difference. The folktale epilogue reinstates Job's status and fortunes; the blameless man prospers, as is proper according to traditional wisdom. Thus traditional wisdom is reaffirmed, but in the world of fantasy! The world in which the righteous prosper is pronounced unreal, and orthodox reality becomes the fairytale ending. We leave the book of Job feeling cheated, but this, I think, is intentional. It is traditional wisdom that has failed us, and thus the story of Job accomplishes its purpose.

Having given a broad overview of my understanding of the book of Job, I would like to raise two issues specific to the *śāṭān*. It has often been remarked that the Joban *śāṭān* plays no role outside of the prologue, an observation used to bolster the claim that the prologue and dialogues are ill-fitted together.[34] I will argue that the *śāṭān* puts in several

----

34. Hoffman, "Prologue and Speech Cycles," 162.

appearances in the poetic sections of the book of Job, albeit appearances cloaked in the guise of irony. Secondly, I will argue that these appearances function to criticize what is conventionally called the religion of the personal god,[35] and in doing so was consistent with a stream of thought in ancient Near Eastern wisdom literature that exalted cosmic, transcendent deity over personal deity. In that these claims rest on the recognition that irony plays a major part in a full appreciation of the book of Job, I will first discuss irony in general, and then offer examples of passages in which an appreciation of irony enriches our understanding of the book of Job.

Irony, in its most basic sense, feeds on the juxtaposition of opposites. It reflects a disparity between the ideal and the actual, between pretense and reality. In the book of Job the audience is confronted with two competing views of reality. On the one hand there is the prologue, which explains Job's misfortunes by recourse to a legal accusation in the divine assembly. On the other hand is traditional wisdom, which explains misfortune by claiming a causal relationship between sin and suffering. The actors in the dialogue, uninformed of the celestial machinations leading to Job's plight, do not perceive the irony, but the audience, privy to the prologue, is confronted with competing explanations of Job's reality. It is this gap between the knowledge of the audience and that of the performers

----

35. Cf. Rainer Albertz, _Persönliche Frömmigkeit und offizielle Religion_ (Stuttgart: Calwer, 1978), Thorkild Jacobsen, _Treasures of Darkness_ (New Haven: Yale, 1976) 147-164, and Hermann Vorlander, _Mein Gott: Die Vorstellungen vom persönlichen Gott im Alten Orient und im Alten Testament_ (AOAT 23; Neukirchen-Vluyn: Neukirchener, 1975).

that paves the way for irony.[36] Thus the potential for irony is embedded in the book's very structure.

Earlier in this chapter, I offered the example of the image of the hedge. In 1:10 the accuser claims that Yahweh surrounds Job with a protective hedge, yet Job in 3:23 perceives Yahweh's hedge as the cause of his sufferings. Job is not aware of the irony of his statement, but the audience, privy to a competing view of reality, could not help but see, in my estimation, the irony of Job's statement. Given the proximity of chapter three to the prologue and the specificity of the image, it seems clear that the book fully intends its audience to perceive Job's statement as ironic.

As I have said, the Joban prologue presents a view of reality inconsistent with traditional wisdom, thus laying the groundwork for potential irony. In 8:20, Bildad offers a conventional truth when he states that God does not reject someone *tām*, "blameless." The obvious implication of Bildad's statement is that Job cannot be *tām*, else he would not be suffering, yet the first thing the audience learns about Job is that he is *tām* (1:1). Again, two competing claims on reality are juxtaposed for the audience, and Bildad's claim, exposed as pretense by the audience's knowledge of the prologue, strikes an ironic note.

Further examples of irony can be perceived in the book's use of rhetorical questions. In 8:3 Bildad asks: "Does God pervert justice, or does Shaddai twist what is right?"[37] Similarly, in 22:4 Eliphaz asks Job:

----

36. Habel, *Job*, 51-52.

37. *haʾēl yĕʿawwēt mišpāṭ wĕʾim-šadday yĕʿawwēt-ṣedeq.*

"Is it because you fear him that he reproves you, enters into judgment with you?"[38] In the reality perceived by Bildad and Eliphaz, the obvious answer to both of these questions is "no," but from the audience's vantage point, which includes the prologue, the answer is not nearly so clear. In the former example, Bildad unwittingly stumbles upon the precise issue in question; thus the "no" he anticipates as a matter of course is far from a matter of course for the audience. In the latter example, the expected answer is also far from clear. In one sense, it is precisely because God has identified Job as an exemplary worshipper that he has been singled out for misfortune, thus turning the anticipated "no" of tradition into an ironic "yes." In another sense, it is the very motivation for Job's fear of God that is being tested, and thus the answer is, for the audience, still ambiguous. In either case the expected response is not forthcoming, and the question itself is ironic in light of the prologue.

Finally, in 22:3 Eliphaz poses this question: "Does Shaddai take delight if you are righteous, or pleasure if your ways are perfect?"[39] This question is intended to be answered in the negative (cf. 35:5-8); according to traditional wisdom, Yahweh's impartiality in judgment is guaranteed by the fact that human actions have no direct impact on him. Yet again, in light of Yahweh's delight in Job expressed in the prologue (1:8), the audience knows that the anticipated "no" of traditional wisdom must in fact be answered "yes."

----

38. hĕmiyyir ʾātĕkā yōkîhekā yābôʾ ʿimmĕkā bammišpāṭ.

39. haḥēpeṣ lĕšadday kî tiṣdāq wĕʾim beṣaʿ kî tattēm dĕrākêkā.

The above examples are but a few of the many that could be used to illustrate the potential for irony implicit in the story of Job. Having briefly demonstrated a few instances of statements in the dialogues that the audience, with their view of the prologue, might very well perceive as ironic, I shall now illustate how irony conjures up the prologue's śāṭān. My examination will focus on four chapters: 9, 16, 19, and 33.

In chapter 9, Job asserts the impossibility of a mere mortal bringing God to trial (vv 2-3). God is both the creator and master of the earth (vv 5-10) and is therefore too powerful to challenge (v 12). Because of this disparity in power between the mortal and the divine, legal redress is impossible (v 32). At this point, Job interjects a hypothetical solution to the dilemma (v 33):

> lūʾ[40] yēš bênēnû môkîaḥ yāšēt yādô ʿal-šěnênû
>
> Would that there were a môkîaḥ between us, so that he could lay his hand on both of us.

Given the imbalance of power between the human and the divine, Job wishes there were a mediating figure who could exert power over both God and himself (v 33). Scholars have translated môkîaḥ variously as "umpire,"[41]

----

40. MT reads lōʾ, but lōʾ yēš is impossible Hebrew; the negative of yēš is ʾên. Thirteen Hebrew MSS, LXX eithe, and the Syriac support the vocalization lūʾ (Driver and Gray, Job, vol. 2, 61). Furthermore, lōʾ yēš is found nowhere else in the Hebrew Bible; lū yēš is found in Num 22:29 and Job 16:4. The spelling with aleph, vocalized lūʾ yēš, can be found in 2 Sam 18:12, 19:17.

41. Pope, Job, 76.

"arbiter,"[42] and "impartial judge,"[43] all of which are fair translations. A môkîaḥ can be described fundamentally as someone who tells the truth regardless of how unpleasant that truth might be (Amos 5:10). If this truth teller happens to be a prophet transmitting God's word to a rebellious Israel, as in the case of Ezekiel (3:26), môkîaḥ can be translated "reprover." If the context is justice at the gate, where impartiality is a supreme virtue (Prov 25:23), and the truth teller is one of the judges, "impartial judge" or the like is a legitimate rendering. Given that Job is envisaging a forensic confrontation, and that he describes the hypothetical môkîaḥ as a being who could exert power over both parties, "impartial judge," "arbiter," and "umpire" are all acceptable translations. However we should keep in mind that a môkîaḥ is, at base, a purveyor of truth.

Job, then, longs for a being who could take both himself and God to task within the context of a trial. From Job's point of view, this being is non-existent; lūʾ yēš, "would that," introduces a statement contrary to fact. But, as the book of Job demonstrates again and again, what is considered fact by the actors in the dialogue is not the same reality as that enjoyed by the audience, privy as they are to the prologue.[44] We have seen, in the example of the hedge, that Job as well as his three friends is capable of

----

42. Habel, Job, 196.

43. Gordis, Job, 111.

44. Previous treatments of this and the other three "mediator passages" in chapters 16, 19 and 33 overlook the disparity between what the audience knows and what Job knows, and it is this failure to recall the prologue when reading these passages that has led scholarship to neglect the irony of Job's wish for a mediator.

misperceiving his situation. I propose that once again, in this passage, Job has misunderstood the mechanics of his degradation. Job's fervent plea is for a truth teller, a m̱ôḵîaḥ, someone who could legally lay his hand on both God and humankind. Alas, he says, no such being exists. But the audience knows better. Not only does such a being exist, he's the one who has gotten Job into his present fix. The m̱ôḵîaḥ, ironically, is the śāṭān, the one who pointed out the potential fault in Yahweh's world order and thus initiated Job's suffering.

The m̱ôḵîaḥ is not the only mask behind which the audience can catch a glimpse of the prologue's celestial accuser. Entering back into the world of the dialogues and moving ahead seven chapters (ch. 16), we once again encounter Job describing to his friends how he has been savaged by God in spite of his blamelessness (vv 6-17). Although no one on earth will vouch for his innocence, he cries (vv 19-21):

> Surely my witness is in the heavens,
> and my observer is on high.
> My interpreter is my friend[a] before God,
> (it is) unto him[b] my eye drips.[c]
> He argues[d] on behalf of a man with God
> (as) a human being (would)[e] for his friend.

a. I am positing, with the majority of modern commentators, that MT m̆ĕlîṣay rēᶜāy is incorrectly pointed.[45] My translation is informed by recognizing that Job in this passage is appealing to a heavenly

----

45. For a comprehensive list of the various emendations and translations that have been proposed, see Curtis ("Job's Witness," n. 7, 552-553).

intercessor who will take his case before God.[46] I reject the notion, put forward for example by Gordis[47] and Dhorme,[48] that no intercessor is referred to in this passage, but rather that Job is fleeing from one conception of God and into the awaiting arms of God the merciful witness. As Samuel Terrien,[49] for instance, points out, verse 21 makes this interpretation impossible. Pope's translation,[50] "interpreter of my thoughts to God," is attractive, but because it involves unnecessary emendation of the consonantal text (i.e. deletion of the final yōd of mlyṣy) I have opted for the translation given above. Furthermore, reading "my friend" rather than "my thoughts" serves to set up a contrast between the terrestrial and celestial spheres. Job has just upbraided his terrestrial friends, calling them "sorrowful comforters" (16:2) who have no sympathy for his position (16:4). In response to his earthly friends, who are not playing the part very well, Job calls upon a celestial friend.[51]

b. The Greek pros Kyrion enanti de autou stazoi mou hē ophthalmos suggests that ʾlyw may have dropped out of MT. This haplography is understandable, as *ʾlyw would have

----

46. S. Mowinckel, "Hiob's gōʾēl und Zeuge im Himmel," BZAW 41 (1925) 210; Nils Johansson, Parakletoi (Lund: Gleerup, 1940) 22-31; Pope, Job, 125-126; Habel, Job, 265.

47. Job, 527.

48. Paul Dhorme, Le livre de Job (Paris: J. Gabalda, 1926) 217.

49. Job, 141.

50. Job, 122.

51. Cf. Habel, Job, 275.

followed *ʾl ʾlwh*.[52]

c. Note the similar image in the "Lament over the Destruction of Ur," l. 145:[53] "To Anu the water of my eye verily I poured."

d. The verb here, *ykḥ*, is the same root as the hiphil participle *môkîaḥ* that was encountered in 9:33. On the basis of this relationship Habel,[54] for example, claims that the *mēlîṣ* of verse 20 should also be understood as an impartial judge, and is the same figure as the *môkîaḥ* of 9:33. I have three objections to equating these terms. First, as I have already demonstrated, a *môkîaḥ* need not be a judge; it is the context in 9:33, and not the inherent meaning of the word, which makes "impartial judge" an appropriate translation in chapter nine. Secondly, B. Gemser[55] has convincingly shown that the verb *ykḥ* can be used to describe a variety of actions performed by various actors in a legal dispute. And finally, Job has already discounted the existence of a *môkîaḥ* able to bring God to task. How then could the *mēlîṣ* whom Job calls upon be the same character as the one he pronounced nonexistent? We must separate these two figures in order to avoid the illogical conclusion, drawn, for example by Pope,[56] that the figure whose existence Job denies in 9:33 is the same figure he appeals to with high expectations in 16:19-21. Nor need

----

52. Habel, *Job*, 266. For other suggestions, see Mowinckel ("Hiob's gōʾēl," 210-211).

53. *ANET*, 458.

54. *Job*, 275-276.

55. "The Rîb Pattern," 124-125, n. 4.

56. *Job*, 126.

we infer, as Habel does,[57] that in the trial Job envisages in chapter 16, the witness is also the arbiter.

e. We can either understand the comparative here as implicit, or read, with a few MSS, *ûbên* for MT *ûben*.

For those modern scholars who see in this passage not a fleeing from God to God but rather reference to a third party, the witness *cum* intermediary is a sympathetic figure who will substantiate Job's claim to blamelessness in front of the heavenly tribunal.[58] Indeed, given that Job is invoking this figure, and given that his goal is to be acquitted, we must certainly agree that, from Job's point of view, the witness is envisaged as a favorable one. But again, Job's reality is not the same as the audience's reality. From the point of view of Job's reality, "witness" implies "favorable witness," "interpreter" implies "favorable interpreter," and so on. But if we pay close attention to the Hebrew terms that Job uses to describe his envisioned intermediary, we realize that these terms are entirely ambiguous. A witness (*ʿēd, śāhēd*) need not be a favorable witness,[59] nor need a *mēlîṣ*, an interpreter or adviser,[60] act in a positive manner (Isa 43:27). Furthermore, the line that I have translated as "he argues *on behalf of* a man with

----

57. *Job*, 275.

58. For example, Mowinckel ("Hiob's gōʾēl," 208).

59. Cf. Tur-Sinai (*Job*, 269), who notes that the witness could be a hostile witness, although he thinks that this hostile witness is God.

60. For *mlṣ* in Phoenician and Punic inscriptions, see Jean and Hoftijzer (*Dictionnaire des inscriptions sémitiques de l'Ouest* [Leiden: Brill, 1960] 138). Unfortunately, the inscriptional evidence does not add to our knowledge of the word's meaning.

God" could equally well be understood as "he argues *against* a man with God," given the ambiguity of the preposition *l*. And finally, Job compares this intermediary's action to that which a human being would undertake on behalf a friend, a *rēaᶜ*. Yet even this statement is double-edged. The only friends we meet in the dialogue are the very ones who forsake Job, arguing against him rather than for him. Thus although Job, on the face of it, is invoking a sympathetic advocate at the heavenly court, the audience, privy to the prologue, might well realize that once again reality has been misperceived. Job believes that right now, *gam ᶜattâ hinnēh* (16:19), there exists a heavenly advocate who could bring his case before God. What he doesn't understand is that he is already on trial, and that his trial has been prompted by a witness, an intermediary, of a different disposition. Job is right, there *is* a witness in the heavens, but that witness has accused him, not supported him. That witness is the *śāṭān* and, like his friends on earth, his celestial "friend" is unconvinced of his true piety. Job has not penetrated the true identity of his heavenly witness, but the audience knows only too well who has been playing the role of interpreter between the mundane and heavenly spheres. Amongst the entire gathering of celestial beings only one besides Yahweh has spoken, and that being is the *śāṭān*.[61]

----

61. By saying that the celestial witness *cum* intermediary is the *śāṭān*, I am not implying that no positive mediating figure existed in Israelite religious tradition. What I am saying is that if we take the prologue scene of the book of Job as our exclusive (non-traditional) reference point, there is only one vocal witness other than Yahweh, and that is the *śāṭān*.

The next passage in which modern scholarship has detected a third party mediating between Job and God is 19:25-27. This passage can lay claim to being one of the most vexing and least well understood passages in the entire Hebrew Bible; already in 1905, Julius Speer[62] could write 93 pages on the variety of interpretations that had been proposed. Much of the literature since that time has retrodden paths already explored, although a few fruitful suggestions have been made.[63] The passage is still far from being solved, and indeed may be corrupt beyond recovery. For this reason, I can not offer an interpretation of 19:25-27 that is as coherent as those offered for 9:33 and 16:19-21. Rather, I shall attempt to establish the general gist of the passage, and then suggest how it might fit into the interpretive framework established for chapters 9 and 16.

As Nils Johansson[64] has noted, chapter 19 is structured very much the same as chapter 16. Both open with Job's peroration against the unsympathetic position his friends have adopted toward him (16:1-5; 19:1-5), followed by an assertion that God has set into motion an unwarranted and horrifying attack on Job, his beleaguered servant (16:6-17; 19:6-22). Job responds with a cry for justice, expressed in 16:18 by his plea that the earth not cover his blood, and in 19:23-24 by his wish to have his words preserved forever in stone. In 16:19-21 this wish is followed by invocation of a heavenly witness and so, argues Johansson, it is reasonable to suspect that

----

62. "Zur Exegese von Hiob 19,25-27," _ZAW_ 25 (1905) 47-140.

63. See below.

64. _Parakletoi_, 32-33.

19:25-27 contains a similar plea.

The MT of 19:25-27 is as follows:

waʾănî yādaʿtî gōʾălî ḥāy
wĕʾaḥărôn ʿal-ʿāpār yāqûm
wĕʾaḥar ʿôrî niqqĕpû-zōʾt
ûmibbĕśārî ʾeḥĕzeh ʾĕlôah
ʾăšer ʾănî ʾeḥĕzeh-llî wĕʿênay rāʾû
wĕlōʾ-zār kālû kilyōtay bĕḥēqî

The first verse is relatively clear: "I know my avenger/redeemer lives, and finally he will stand up upon my grave.". Like all translations of this famous verse, this one involves some reading into the text. M. L. Barré has argued that, in Hebrew and Aramaic, all instances of the formulaic pair ḥyh//qwm have as their *Sitz im Leben* healing or resurrection.[65] I do not wish to discuss at this time Barré's overall thesis, but rather provide additional support for his contention that Job 19:25 deals with divine healing. In vv 8-20, Job enumerates the repercussions that divine disfavor has effected in his life. Job has lost his high social status (v 9), has been abandoned by both friends and kin alike (vv 13-14), is held in contempt by his slaves and reviled by urchins (vv 15-16, 18), and finally beset by rotting flesh (v 20). Both the pattern and many of the particulars of Job's plight can be paralleled in the Babylonian *Ludlul bēl nēmeqi*, a composition widely acknowledged to exhibit points of contact with the book of Job. The sufferer in *Ludlul*, Šubše-mešrê-šakkan, also catalogues the woes that had befallen him as a result of

----

65. M. L. Barré, "A Note on Job 19:25," *VT* 29 (1979) 107. On the basis of this observation, Barre reads the verb ḥyh for MT ḥāy, an emendation with which I do not agree.

losing divine favor. In tablet 1, he too complains of his loss of social status (1.75-78; cf. 1.103-104):

> My mighty chest, a little child pushed away,
> My sides, which used to stride along, now grasped each other.
> As one who used to walk nobly about, I had to slink along;
> I was magnificent, but turned into a slave.[66]

Directly thereafter, the sufferer complains that family and friends had deserted him (1.79, 84-85):

> To my extended family I had become like an unattached person...
> My brother became a stranger to me,
> My close friend became a wretch and a devil.[67]

From a new fragment[68] we learn that the sufferer's abandonment by family and friends was followed by the derision of his servants (1.89-90):

> My servant cursed me publicly,
> My servant girl insulted me in front of the people.

Finally, having catalogued the various social ills that had befallen him, the sufferer turns to his physical ailments, which he describes at great length (2.49-107). Totally debilitated, he describes the state to which he had come (2.114-115):

----

66. A transliteration of the Akkadian text can be found in W. G. Lambert, Babylonian Wisdom Literature (Oxford, 1959) 34.

67. For the transliterated text, see Lambert (BWL, 34).

68. BM 61433, published by E. Leichty, Essays on the Ancient Near East in Memory of Jacob Joel Finkelstein, 145.

> The grave was open, my funerary goods ready,
> Before I was dead the mourning for me was already finished.[69]

The scene here envisioned in _Ludlul_ is paralleled closely by a text discovered at Ras Shamra[70] and usually dubbed "The Righteous Sufferer" (ll. 10'-17'):

> My family was gathered around, to _embalm_ before my time;
> My household was drawn near, present for dark grief.
> My brothers, like frenzied prophets,
> were bathed in their own blood,
> My sisters poured on me the _purest_ oil,
> Until my master raised my head,
> Gave life to me the dead,
> Until Marduk my master raised my head,
> Gave life to me the dead.[71]

Like the Ras Shamra fragment, the sufferer in _Ludlul_ has reached his very grave. It is at this point that the deity finally intervenes, to veritably snatch the sufferer from the grave, the open maw of death.[72]

----

69. The transliterated text can be found in Lambert (_BWL_, 46).

70. Jean Nougayrol, _Ugaritica_ _V_, Mission de Ras Shamra, tome 16 (Paris: Imprimerie Nationale, 1968) no. 162.

71. Translated by William Moran, unpublished notes, 1983. The underlined words represent conjectural translations.

72. The beginning of tablet 3 of _Ludlul_ is, unfortunately, broken. However, when the text becomes clear, the sufferer is informed in a series of three visions that Marduk has delivered him from his malady (3.1-44). At the beginning of tablet 4 (line 6) we learn that this rescue was from the burial pit.

For the _topos_ of rescue _in extremis_, cf. William Moran ("Notes on the Hymn to Marduk in _Ludlul bēl Nēmeqi_," _JAOS_ 103 [1981] 258).

In the book of Job, *ʿāpār*, "dust," is used several times to refer to the grave and/or the netherworld that lies on the other side of it (17:16, 20:11, 21:26). Given both the structural and contextual similarities of Job 19 and *Ludlul bēl nēmeqi*, I understand 19:25b to mean that Job, like his Babylonian counterpart, expects to be rescued from the very jaws of death.

The following verses (26-27) are too obscure for coherent translation. If I have understood verse 25 correctly, 26b seems to say "and from my flesh [i.e. while still alive] I will have a vision of God."[73] Verse 27 seems to restate Job's belief that he will see God for himself (*ʾḥzh-ly*), the contemplation of which causes his insides to quake (*klw klyty bḥqy*).

One of the many topics of debate in this passage is the identity of the *gōʾēl*, the avenger or redeemer. Gordis,[74] for instance, insists that the redeemer is God, the same God as the one responsible for Job's torment. For Gordis, 19:23-29 evidences Job's growing faith in the underlying rightness of the universe:[75] at first, Job wishes for an impartial arbiter (9:33), then becomes certain that he has a heavenly witness (16:19), and finally affirms an avenging

----

73. Verse 26a seems hopelessly corrupt. Johansson (*Parakletoi*, 33-34) proposes reading *nzqp-ʾty* for the enigmatic MT *nqpw-zʾt*, but offers no justification; Janzen (*Job*, 142-143) suggests *nqp* II; Mowinckel ("Hiob's gōʾēl," 212) pronounces the phrase "totally senseless." William Irwin ("Job's Redeemer," *JBL* 81 [1962] 217) leaves the phrase untranslated.

74. *Job*, 526-529.

75. Gordis, *Job*, 526.

vindicator (19:25). Gordis supports his argument by claiming that, unlike a human court in which there is a division of roles, this division "...is superfluous in the heavenly assize, where all the functions are performed by God.".[76] This claim, however, quickly loses force when we recall that in the prologue itself there is more than one actor in the heavenly court; in addition to Yahweh there is a celestial accuser.[77] Furthermore, Gordis overlooks the clear statement in 16:21 that the witness will argue for a man with God; if the witness is also God, is this not an unnecessary contradiction?

Given that 16:19-21 clearly envisages a witness/intermediary who acts on humankind's behalf in front of God, given the parallels in both structure and content between chapters 16 and 19, and given the fact that Job perceives God as his enemy, it seems more likely that the gōʾēl whom Job affirms as his rescuer from death should be understood as a being distinct from the God who is tormenting him.[78] Job is affirming, then, that a heavenly redeemer will save his life, interposing between himself and the grave. Again, I would propose that this description ironically conjures up the prologue. Job may be looking forward to intervention by a third party who will prove to be his ultimate salvation from the grave, but the audience knows that the only active divine third party is seeking to drive Job to his grave, not rescue

----

76. Gordis, Job, 526.

77. Cf. Habel, Job, 275.

78. Additional support for this interpretation is provided by 33:23-25, which is treated below. Note also Gen 48:16, which speaks of "the messenger who redeems me from all evil," hammalʾāk haggōʾēl ʾōtî mikkol-rāʿ.

him from it.[79]

The final passage I would like to treat is located in the Elihu speeches of chapters 32-37. In chapter 33 Elihu asserts that he is speaking knowledgeably (v 3), but because he like Job is mortal, Job should not feel intimidated about responding to his accusations (vv 4-7). Elihu rejects Job's claim to purity (vv 8-12), and insists that God *does* answer human charges, although humankind may not perceive God's speech (vv 13-14). God may chose to speak in night visions (vv 15-18) or through sickness, a physical chastisement that can take a person to the very edge of death (vv 19-22). Thus poised at the graveside, Elihu pictures the following scene in the divine assembly (vv 23-25):

> If he [a man] has a messenger,
> An intermediary, one in a thousand
> To speak for a man's uprightness,
> Who has mercy on him and says, "Spare[a] him
> from going down to the Pit,
> I have found a ransom."
> Then his flesh becomes fresher[b] than in youth,
> He returns to the days of his vigor.[c]

a. *pdʿ*, an otherwise unattested root, is widely acknowledged to be a scribal error either for *pdh*,

----

79. It is possible that the enigmatic reference to Job's skin (*ʿôrî*)in 19:26a was designed to direct the audience's attention specifically to the prologue's second interaction between Yahweh and the *śāṭān*. When Yahweh observes that Job has remained blameless in spite of the accuser's initial onslaught (2:3), the *śāṭān* responds by threatening Job's life (2:4). "Skin for skin" (*ʿôr bĕʿad ʿôr*) he says; "all that a man has he will give for his life." A connection between 19:26a and the second interchange between Yahweh and the accuser has been perceived also by T. J. Meek ("Job 19:25-27," *VT* 6 [1956] 102), who understands the verb *ngpw* in relation to the skin disease imposed upon Job by the accuser (2:7).

"redeem," or pr^{c}, "let loose; spare." I have preferred the latter due to the possibility of scribal confusion between dālet and rēš.[80]

b. The hapax rṭpš has been much discussed, but none of the proposed solutions inspires philological conviction. Both the context and the parallel colon strongly suggest rejuvenation, and "fresh" is but one of the many adequate suggestions.[81] I have translated "fresher," taking the min of minnō^{c}ar as a comparative.

c. Note that this passage as a whole, depicting as it does a divine intermediary who snatches the sufferer from the Pit, tends to confirm my interpretation of 19:25.

Elihu claims to be privy to the workings of the divine sphere, yet, ironically, the scene he describes is precisely the opposite of the assembly scenes known to the audience. At a gathering of the gods, only one of the many has spoken to interpret a man's actions to Yahweh. Indeed, the subject addressed is a man's uprightness, but the intermediary speaks not in support of Job's uprightness, but rather to challenge his motivation. And rather than effecting a sick man's rescue from the Pit and restoration to health, the intermediary's intervention launches a healthy and prosperous man on a quest for death and oblivion (ch. 3).[82]

----

80. Habel, Job, 458.

81. Habel, Job, 458.

82. Kissane (Job, 225) notes that 19:23 offers the same conception of God's dealings with men as that which underlies the prologue. Whereas I think Kissane is right to read 19:23-25 in light of the prologue, he has failed to notice that 19:23-25 envisages a scenario diametrically opposed to the revealed workings of the divine council, and therefore fails to notice the irony.

In the four chapters treated above, I have argued that the figures of the hoped-for arbiter, the benevolent intermediary, and the redeeming *gōʾēl* should be understood ironically. Because the audience has been confronted with two opposing explanations of reality (i.e. that posited by the prologue and that claimed by the actors who have no knowledge of the prologue), much of what the dialogue's characters assert as true is perceived by the audience as being clearly false. Although the most obvious examples of this tension come from the speeches of the friends, whose traditional answers do not penetrate the mechanics of Job's suffering, the example of the hedge demonstrates that Job, too, is capable of ironically misperceiving reality. Thus when Job expresses his desire for a *mōkîaḥ* who could lay his hand on both himself and God, a wish he sees as incapable of fulfillment, Job has once again misperceived the dynamics of his degradation. Ironically a *mōkîaḥ* does exist, but he is the very being who has landed Job in his current predicament. This same being has witnessed against him, claiming that in a world order that necessarily rewards piety, piety itself must be suspect. He has functioned as an interpreter of a man's actions to God, but his interpretation has not been salvific, as Job had supposed it would be. The prologue's only active intermediary has spoken to his detriment rather than his betterment, launching Job toward death rather than saving him from it.

In support of this interpretation, I offer the following observation. The problem of Job's suffering is ultimately resolved *not* through the intervention of some mediating figure, but rather through Yahweh's appearance in the stormwind. The friends have tried to act as interpreters of the divine world through the agency of traditional wisdom, but they have failed. Elihu himself notes their failure, chiding them for not successfully playing the role of *môkîaḥ* (32:12). Elihu claims to pick up the interpretive torch from the failing hands of the three friends (32:10, 12), but he too effects no reconciliation. The human mediators have failed, and so, I would argue, has the metaphor of the divine mediator. Resolution occurs when Yahweh appears in the whirlwind, an act precipitated *not* by a celestial mediator, but by Job's invocation of a self-curse.[83] The book of Job, then, effectively rejects the notion of an efficacious divine intermediary who prompts the high god to act on humankind's behalf.

When Sigmund Mowinckel first proposed understanding the *mēlîṣ* of chapter 16 and the *gōʾēl* of chapter 19 as divine third party figures, he equated their role with that of the personal god in Mesopotamian religious tradition.[84] As both Thorkild Jacobsen[85] and Hermann Vorlander[86] have demonstrated, one of the functions of the personal god was to intercede for his or her client in the divine assembly.[87] If a person fell ill or suffered some other misfortune, it was thought that the person had somehow offended his or her personal

----

83. Robertson, "Job," 461; Good, "Job," 475-476.

84. Mowinckel, "Hiob's gōʾēl," 211.

85. *The Treasures of Darkness*, 159-160.

86. *Mein Gott*, 4, 22, 87-90.

87. It is difficult to directly equate the Mesopotamian personal god with the biblical divine mediator because we are moving from a polytheistic to a monolatrous society. What I am suggesting is a *functional* equivalence in that the Mesopotamian personal god and the biblical advocate take their client's side in the heavenly court.

god.[88] Thus sin, an offense against the personal god, was causally tied to misfortune in the life experience of the individual. We can detect here the speculative basis upon which a universe operating on the principle of just retribution is founded. A causal link is established between individual piety and just reward. Fulfill the necessary obligations, and prosperity inevitably results.

It is precisely to this conception of an inevitably retributive universe that the Joban *śāṭān* objects. It has been widely noted that the god who confronts Job from the whirlwind is a cosmic god, who ignores Job's plea for justice and simply demands worship based on brute force and acknowledged but unexplained mystery. The book of Job rings the death knell for personal retributive justice, at least for those who subscribe to its message. The personal god is dead; the metaphor of benevolent intermediary has failed.

The book of Job is not the only work in the ancient Near East that addresses the issue of the relationship between the religion of the personal god and transcendent, cosmic deity. Although personal god religion classically stated depicted an efficacious personal deity to whom the client could appeal for representation of his or her case in the celestial assembly, *Ludlul bēl nēmeqi* portrays a very different situation.[89] In *Ludlul*, we are repeatedly told that the

----

88. See, for example, *Ludlul bēl nēmeqi* 2.10-22, and the Babylonian theodicy (Lambert, *BWL*, 63-89) 2.21.

89. The ensuing discussion owes a debt to William Moran, who suggested to me that *Ludlul* reflects the rethinking of personal god religion in light of an all-powerful Marduk.

personal deities' disposition toward their client is totally dependent on the all-powerful Marduk's disposition. Rather than influence the celestial powers at the divine bar, the personal god acts entirely in accord with Marduk's wishes (1.15-16):

> When he [Marduk] looks with disfavor,
> šēdu and lamassu go far away,
> But when he looks favorably at he whom he rejected,
> his personal god returns.

This attitude is expressed again, in 1.41-46:

> From the day the Lord became angry with me,
> And warrior Marduk became enraged with me,
> My personal god cast me away, disappeared forever,
> My goddess went away, far far away.
> He sundered the good šēdu from my side,
> Frightened off my lamassu so that she went looking for another.

In *Ludlul*, then, the personal god is no longer, at least in some circles, the vehicle of propitiation. I would suggest that the book of Job presents a similar state of affairs. Although Job calls upon the agency of a divine intercessor, none is forthcoming. Instead, Job encounters deity in its cosmic aspect,[90] and is forced to deal with this deity in cosmic rather than personal terms. By doing so, Job accepts his rightful place in relationship to universal deity, and individual justice becomes the storybook ending.

----

90. The personal god was not necessarily a "lesser" god; deities such as Marduk, Sin, Adad and Anu could also be personal gods (Albertz, *Persönliche Frömmigkeit*, 101-139). The difference is the individual's perception of the relationship in which he or she stands to a particular deity (Jacobsen, *Treasures*, 147).

Chapter 6

THE *śāṭān* IN ZECHARIAH 3

The next occurrence of a celestial *śāṭān* to be investigated appears in the collection of materials stemming from the prophet Zechariah (Zech 1-8), whose prophecies are dated to the second year of the reign of Darius (Zech 1:7), or 520 B.C.E..[1] The collection contains eight night visions with accompanying oracular material. The fourth vision, Zech 3:1-10, features the high priest Joshua standing in front of the *malʾāk yhwh* with the *śāṭān* on his right, poised to accuse him. Before we turn to the scene itself, some preliminary matters must be discussed. First, we must determine whether 3:1-10 was originally a single unit. Then we must address the question of whether Zechariah 3 is a later addition to the vision cycle. Both of these questions call for a brief overview of the restoration program envisaged by Zechariah.

Central to Zechariah's program for a rejuvenated Judah and Jerusalem was the rebuilding of the Jerusalem temple. Although temple reconstruction may have begun ca. 538 B.C.E. with the permission of Cyrus (Ezra 6:2-5) and under the direction of Sheshbazzar (Ezra

----

1. The text dates all eight visions to a single day in the second year of Darius' reign. For evidence that this is an artificial construct, see Alfred Jepsen ("Kleine Beiträge zum Zwölfprophetenbuch III: 4.Sacharja," *ZAW* 20 [1945-1948] 99).

5:7-17),[2] Zechariah credits the Davidide Zerubbabel with laying the foundation of the second temple (Zech 4:9).[3] From the earliest level of materials preserved in Zechariah 1-8 we learn that the prophet envisaged a diarchy of priestly and royal rule, the latter element perhaps being encouraged by the widespread rebellions that accompanied Darius' accession to the Persian throne.[4] The fifth vision (4:1-6aα, 10b-14) features a menorah mystically infused with the divine presence[5]

----

2. Cf. Frank Moore Cross, "A Reconstruction of the Judean Restoration," *JBL* 94 (1975) 12 n. 43, 15.

3. The apparent contradiction of the biblical sources concerning who began temple reconstruction has prompted A. Gelston ("The Foundations of the Second Temple," *VT* 16 [1966] 232-235) to suggest that *ysd* need not necessarily mean "found," but can also mean "rebuild." Other scholars, for example Kurt Galling (*Studien zur Geschichte Israels im persischen Zeitalter* [Tübingen: J.C.B. Mohr, 1964] 134) and Karl Beyse (*Serubbabel und die Königserwartungen der Propheten Haggai und Sacharja* [Stuttgart: Calwer, 1972] 27), suggest that the rebuilding effort initiated by Sheshbazzar did not enjoy popular support and thus was either ignored or aborted. The later rebuilding campaign mounted under Joshua and Zerubbabel did result in the completion of the new temple, and therefore it could be said that Zerubbabel laid its foundations.

4. See, for example, David Peterson, *Haggai and Zechariah 1-8: A Commentary* (OTL; Philadelphia: Westminster, 1984) 23. Zechariah's contemporary, the prophet Haggai, informs us that Zerubbabel held an office (*peḥâ*) within the Persian administration (1:1), but that when Yahweh overthrows the "throne of kingdoms" (*kissēʾ mamlākôt*), Zerubbabel will become a "seal" or "signet ring" (*ḥōtām*, 2:22-23). I understand the "throne of kingdoms" to be Persian rule, and the "signet ring" to imply royal office (1 Kgs 21:8).

5. For an excellent discussion of the symbolism involved in this vision, see Susan Niditch (*The Symbolic Vision in Biblical Tradition* [HSM 30; Chico: Scholars, 1980] 101-115). As Niditch (*Vision*, 113) describes it, "a quintessential sign of cult [the menorah] is interpreted

flanked by two olive trees, the anointed royal scion and priest. These two figures[6] were to be crowned (6:9), and the royal "branch" (ṣemaḥ) was to rule from his throne while the priest was to stand at his side in perfect harmony (6:13). Thus Joshua and Zerubbabel, priest and scion of David, would preside over a reconstituted community with the temple at its center, ushering in an age of peace and prosperity.

The idyllic restoration envisaged by Zechariah did not come to pass. Temple building was challenged from without by the Persian governor Tattenai (Ezra 5:3), and from within by factions objecting to various particulars of the Zadokite restoration program.[7] Darius gained firm control over the Persian empire. Zerubbabel disappeared from the stage of history without a trace; we know nothing of his fate. Whatever his end, he certainly did not fulfill the high hopes invested in him through the glowing prophecies of Zechariah. The Zadokite priesthood survived, but aspirations for a Davidic ruler were pushed into the future. With this brief overview in mind, let us turn to Zechariah 3.

> 3 [1]And he showed me Joshua the high priest standing
> in front of the messenger of Yahweh, and the śāṭān
> standing on his right hand side to accuse him.
> [2]And the messenger[a] of Yahweh said to the śāṭān,
> "May Yahweh rebuke you, O accuser; may Yahweh who
> has chosen Jerusalem rebuke you. Isn't this [man]
> a brand rescued from the fire?". [3]Now Joshua was

----

to be an arm of the divine council [eyes of the Lord]."

6. Cf. Paul Hanson, The Dawn of Apocalyptic (Philadelphia: Fortress, 1979) 256.

7. See Hanson, Dawn, 246-247, 254, 261-269.

clothed in filthy garments <while he was standing in front of the messenger>.[b] 4And he [i.e. the *malʾāk yhwh*] answered and said to the ones standing before him, saying: "Take the filthy garments off him, <And he said to him, "See, I have removed your iniquity from you.">[c] and clothe him[d] in pure raiment,[e] 5and < >[f] put a clean turban on his head." And they put a clean turban on his head, and clothed him with clothes <while the messenger of Yahweh stood by>.[g] 6And the messenger of Yahweh adjured Joshua, saying: 7"Thus says Yahweh Sebaot. If you walk in my ways and perform my services, and if[h] you judge my house[i] and keep my courts, then I will give you access among those standing here. 8Hear, Joshua the high priest, you and your compatriots sitting in front of you, for they are a token that I am bringing my servant Branch. 9For the stone that I have set before Joshua, seven eyes upon a single stone, I am hereby engraving its inscription (oracle of Yahweh Sebaot). And I will remove the iniquity of that land in a single day. 10On that day (oracle of Yahweh Sebaot) each of you will call upon his neighbor [to sit together] under vine and fig tree."

a. MT reads *yhwh* rather than *malʾāk yhwh*, but this is difficult because of the following third person statement, "May Yahweh rebuke you." The emendation is proposed many modern commentators.

b. The phrase "while he was standing in front of the messenger" may be a later addition.

c. *wayyōʾmer ʾēlāyw rĕʾēh heʿĕbartî mēʿalêkā ʿăwōnekā* interrupts the series of commands addressed to the divine attendants. It is best understood as an early gloss[8] that clarifies the meaning of Joshua's change of

----

8. So also Johansson, *Parakletoi*, 35.

clothing.

d. MT *wĕhalbēš ʾōtekā* makes little sense. Read with the LXX *kai endusate auton* = *wĕhalbîšû ʾōtô*.

e. D. W. Thomas[9] has convincingly shown, on the basis of Arabic and Akkadian cognates, that *maḥălāṣôt* means "pure (clothing)."

f. Reading, with the LXX, *kai epithete* = *wĕśîmû*, which continues the series of imperatives.[10]

g. The phrase "while the messenger of Yahweh stood by" may be a later addition.

h. I am taking *wĕgam-ʾattâ tādîn ʾet-bêtî wĕgam tišmōr ʾet-ḥăṣērāy* as a continuation of the protasis. The protasis begins with two disjunctive phrases, *ʾim-bidrakāy tēlēk wĕʾim ʾet-mišmartî tišmōr*. The twice repeated *wĕgam* serves to continue the disjunction. The apodosis begins with the converted perfect *wĕnātattî*.[11]

i. Scholars are divided over the meaning of *tādîn ʾet-bêtî*: does it mean "judge my house (= my people)," or "administer my house (= my temple)?" It seems to me that the former option is clearly the correct one. In no other Hebrew Bible text does *dîn* mean "administer." On the contrary, the context is always clearly legal. Furthermore, there is a definite shift in the exilic period toward referring to the Israelites as *bêt yiśrāʾēl* as opposed to the earlier *bĕnê yiśrāʾēl*. The former

----

9. "A Note on *mḥlṣwt* in Zechariah 3:4," *JTS* 33 (1932) 279-280.

10. See Christian Jeremias, *Die Nachtgesichte des Sacharja* (Göttingen: Vandenhoeck und Ruprecht, 1977) 202-203 n. 8.

11. For other arguments in favor of this division between protasis and apodosis, see W. A. M. Beuken (*Haggai-Sacharja 1-8* [Assen: Van Gorcum, 1967] 291-293) and Lars Rignell (*Die Nachtgesichte des Sacharja* [Lund: Ohlssons, 1950] 122-123).

designation is particularly prevalent in Jeremiah (according to BDB, 19 times) and Ezekiel (BDB, 81 times), and is also found three times in Zechariah (8:13, 15, 19). In Ezekiel, Israel is referred to seven times as bêt mĕrî, "a rebellious house," thus demonstrating that bêt could be used without the specification yiśrāʾēl and still convey the meaning "people." On the basis of the lexical evidence, therefore, it seems preferable to understand dîn in the well-established sense of "to judge" rather than the otherwise unattested meaning "to administer," and understand bêtî to mean "my people." The phrase means that the high priest is to ensure that the legislative and forensic responsibilities of the priesthood are properly carried out, namely interpretation of tôrâ (Hag 2:11-13) and the deciding of cases that could not be settled by civil process (Num 5:11-28; 2 Chr 6:22; 19:8-11).

The first issue to settle is whether chapter 3 is all of a piece, or whether we can detect either formal seams or contextual incongruities. Verse 8 begins with an address to Joshua to hear (šĕmaʿ-nāʾ); this new "call to attention" suggests that verse 8 begins a separate unit.[12] Furthermore, Joshua's compatriots of verse 8 (rēʿêkā hayyōšĕbîm lĕpānêkā) introduce a group not present in the scene set in the previous verses.[13] In verses 1-7, the beings standing in attendance (hāʿōmĕdîm lĕpānāyw) are clearly the divine members of the heavenly court, yet surely these divine beings are not the compatriots who are a sign of the coming of Branch. Finally, verses 8-10 are concerned with the laying of the

----

12. Peterson, Zechariah, 208.

13. W. Eichrodt, "Vom Symbol zum Typos," TZ 13 (1957) 510.

foundation stone of the temple,[14] while verses 1-7 are concerned with a different problem, Joshua's suitability for the office of high priest. Thus it seems clear on both formal and contextual grounds that verses 1-7 should be considered apart from verses 8-10.[15] Turning, then, to verses 1-7, the next issue to resolve is the relationship between 3:1-7 and the other seven night visions found in Zechariah 1-8.

Christian Jeremias[16] has assembled the most comprehensive series of arguments for denying Zech 3:1-7 a place in the most primitive vision cycle of Zechariah 1-8.[17] While admitting points of contact between 3:1-7 and the other seven night visions, Jeremias notes the following differences. The vision in Zechariah 3 begins with wyrʾny, a formula which does not introduce any of

----

14. Much has been written about the ʾeben of verse 8. The two principle theories are 1) that it is a (gem)stone in the turban of the high priest, and 2) that it is the foundation stone of the temple. The evidence weighs more heavily in favor of the latter option. The best presentation of the evidence is given by A. Petitjean ("La mission de Zorobabel et la reconstruction du temple: Zach., III, 8-10," ETL 42 [1966] 40-71; Les oracles du proto-Zacherie [Paris: J. Gabalda, 1969] 73-82).

15. Beuken (Sacharja, 290-303) is the primary proponent of the theory that verses 8-10 originally belonged with verses 1-5, and that verses 6-7 are a later insertion. For a refutation of Beuken's position, see Jeremias (Nachtgesichte, 223-225).

16. Nachtgesichte, 201-203.

17. In support of this position, see also Jepsen ("Sacharja," 95-96), Klaus Seybold (Bilder zum Tempelbau [Stuttgart: K.B.W., 1974] 57), Karl Elliger (Die zwölfe kleinen Propheten [Göttingen: Vandenhoeck und Ruprecht, 1975] 120), J. W. Rothstein (Die Nachtgesichte des Sacharja [Leipzig: J. C. Hinrichs, 1910] 102), and Carol L. Meyers and Eric M. Meyers (Haggai, Zechariah 1-8 [AB 25B; Garden City: Doubleday, 1987] 213-215.

the other seven night visions. The *malʾāk dōbēr bî* (or *angelus interpres*), a primary character in the other seven visions, is conspicuously absent. Instead, Zechariah 3 features the *malʾāk yhwh*, who performs a totally different function. Also unlike the other seven visions the prophet asks no question about the significance of what he sees, nor is he quizzed by a celestial figure about the meaning of the vision. Indeed, the prophet is uncharacteristically passive. Also uncharacteristically, the interpretation of the change of clothing is addressed to Joshua,[18] as is the final *Gotteswort*. The highly symbolic content of the other night visions is in chapter 3 replaced by clearly defined characters and objects. And finally, chapter 3 destroys the symmetry of a cycle of seven visions which, without chapter 3, would place the vision of the menorah flanked by the two olive trees, so clearly the central image,[19] in the middle point of the vision cycle.

Jeremias' arguments are for the most part sound[20] and, taken cumulatively, convincing. Those who

----

18. As we have seen above, this interpretation is probably a gloss.

19. See Paul Hanson, "In Defiance of Death: Zechariah's Symbolic Universe," Marvin Pope Festschrift (New Haven: Four Quarters Publishing, forthcoming).

20. My only objection to Jeremias' evidence is that he portrays the other seven night visions as being more consistent with each other than they actually are. For instance, the third vision (2:5-9) describes a man with a measuring cord in his hand. Unlike the vision of the menorah and the olive trees, for example, the man is not a symbol in need of interpretation. There is no interchange between the prophet and the *angelus interpres* about the meaning of the vision; rather, the prophet inquires directly of the man where he is going (2:6). And finally, it is not at all clear who the *angelus interpres* is instructed to speak to in verse 8; does

maintain that 3:1-7 should be included in the original vision cycle[21] typically rehearse these objections, but do not refute them systematically. Beuken[22] and Rudolph[23] account for the absence of the angelus interpres by pointing out that Zechariah recognizes what he sees and therefore no interpretation is necessary, but this observation begs the question of why 3:1-7 is the only vision in which the interpreting messenger is absent. Beuken[24] further suggests that the inclusion of 3:1-7 does not disturb the supposed symmetry of a cycle of seven visions with the important menorah and olive trees vision highlighted in the central position. Rather, he claims that the visions of Zechariah 3 and 4 should be considered a central pair because both feature Joshua and Zerubbabel. To this I have two objections. First, the number seven is widely acknowledged to be a number of completeness in the ancient Semitic world, whereas the number eight did not carry this connotation. Second, Beuken's claim that Zerubbabel is present in the vision of chapter 3 is bound up with his assertion that verses 8-10, which mention Branch, originally belonged with verses 1-5 and formed a single vision.[25] As we have

----

hannaᶜar hallāz refer to the prophet or the man with the measuring cord? However, it should be noted that the man is left unidentified, and the angelus interpres is present. For both of these reasons, 2:5-9 stands closer to the other six night visions than to 3:1-7.

21. For example, Beuken (Sacharja, 282-283), Petersen (Zachariah, 112, 187), and W. Rudolph (Haggai-Sacharja 1-8-Sacharja 9-14-Maleachi [KAT 13; Gütersloh: Gerd Mohn, 1976] 93).

22. Sacharja, 283.

23. Sacharja, 93.

24. Sacharja, 282.

25. Beuken, Sacharja, 290-303.

seen above, both form-critical and contextual observations mitigate against Beuken's position. In short, it is best to regard Zech 3:1-7 as a later insertion into a cycle of seven visions.[26] This is important for our purposes because it means that 3:1-7 is stylistically independent of these visions. Whereas these other visions typically feature a figure that symbolically stands for something else (menorah, olive trees, woman in an ephah, flying scroll), this need not be true for 3:1-7.

In summary of our preliminary findings, Zech 3:1-7 was originally independent of verses 8-10. 3:1-7 addresses the problem of Joshua's suitability for the office of high priest, whereas verses 8-10 are concerned with laying the foundation stone of the temple. Furthermore, 3:1-7 stands outside the primitive cycle of seven visions that described, in highly symbolic terms, Zechariah's conception of a restored community with Yahweh's presence in the temple at its center and a diarchy of priestly and royal rule. It does not share the primary features characteristic of the other seven night visions of Zechariah 1-8, and indeed disturbs a cycle originally constructed to highlight Zechariah's vision of diarchy. The independence of 3:1-7 suggests that it need not be interpreted in the manner of the other seven visions. Unlike, for instance, the woman in the ephah or the menorah flanked by olive trees, Joshua is not a symbol in need of interpretation.

Having established our contextual bearings, let

----

26. This need not imply that 3:1-7 postdates the other seven visions; indeed, its juxtaposition with verses 8-10 may indicate that the issue of Joshua's legitimacy was addressed before temple construction began.

us focus on Zechariah's *śāṭān*. The overwhelming majority of scholars who have worked with Zech 3:1-7 maintain that Joshua is a cypher for the restored community, and that his change of clothes represents the change in the community's status from impure to pure (or sinful to forgiven) in the eyes of Yahweh.[27] The *śāṭān*, they say, is objecting to this change in the community's status. Yahweh wishes to pardon his people; the *śāṭān* is opposed. The *śāṭān*, therefore, represents the strict observance of legality that precludes pardon;[28] he is the relentless accuser who rigidly interprets retributive justice.[29] He is rebuked for trying to obstruct divine mercy.[30] He is opposed to the plan of salvation.[31] He is the justice of Yahweh as contrasted to Yahweh's grace.[32] In what follows, I hope to expose this interpretation as highly fanciful.

Although the other seven night visions require varying levels of interpretation because of their symbolic character, we have seen above that Zech 3:1-7 is different. Unlike the other seven visions, the characters are well known and clearly defined. Also

----

27. For example, Miloš Bič (*Das Buch Sacharja* [Berlin: Evangelische Verlagsanstalt, 1962] 22), Beuken (*Sacharja*, 299), Elliger (*Zwölfe*, 121) and Rignell (*Nachtgesichte*, 101, 105). Jeremias (*Nachtgesichte*, 208) understands Joshua to represent the returning exiles.

28. For example, Marti, "Zwei Studien," 242.

29. For example, Duhm, *Die bösen Geister*, 61.

30. For example, Lods, "Les origines," 650.

31. For example, Kluger, *Satan*, 144.

32. For example, H. G. Mitchell, *Haggai, Zechariah, Malachi and Jonah* (ICC; Edinburgh: T. and T. Clark, 1912) 151.

unlike the other seven visions there is no angelus interpres, a fact which in itself would suggest that the content of Zech 3:1-7 was designed to be self-evident. As we shall see, there is little to be explained but much to be proclaimed[33] in Zech 3:1-7.

What is our passage trying to accomplish? The majority of scholars who have worked on Zech 3:1-7 understand the scene presented to be one of investiture,[34] and I agree. That priestly consecration involved a change of clothes is demonstrated by Exod 29:4 and Lev 8:7; it is also accompanied by the donning of a turban (miṣnepet, Exod 29:6; Lev 8:9). Furthermore, as Bič,[35] Jeremias,[36] and Peterson[37] have observed, Zechariah 3 is drawing on the genre of the prophetic call, a genre which implies a change of role or status. To demonstrate the parallels Jeremias[38] notes the many points of contact between Zech 3:1-7 and Isaiah 6. Both passages depict a human being present at a meeting of the

----

33. I am paraphrasing a comment made by Burke Long ("Reports of Visions Among the Prophets," JBL 95 [1976] 358) to describe the vision-report form in Jeremiah.

34. For example, Bič (Sacharja, 43), Beuken (Sacharja, 284), Herbert May ("A Key to the Interpretation of Zechariah's Visions," JBL 57 [1938] 179), Jeremias (Nachtgesichte, 209) and W. Nowack (Die kleinen Propheten [HKAT; Göttingen: Vandenhoeck and Ruprecht, 1922] 338). Rudolph (Sacharja, 97 n. 15) objects on the basis that Joshua is introduced in verse 1, prior to his donning of fresh garments and turban, as the high priest. I understand this introduction to mean that, for the author of 3:1-7, Joshua's investiture was a fait accompli.

35. Sacharja, 44.

36. Nachtgesichte, 203-205.

37. Zechariah, 207-208.

38. Nachtgesichte, 203-205.

divine council. Both humans are impure, and both are cleansed by a heavenly intermediary. As a result of this action, both characters acquire authority;[39] Isaiah is empowered to deliver God's message, and Joshua gains ongoing access to the divine council. For Jeremias, these parallels are too close and too abundant to be accidental; Zech 3:1-7 must be purposely drawing on the call genre.[40]

Since a call implies the taking on of a new function it is appropriate to understand Joshua's change of clothes as an investiture, a mythologized induction of Joshua into the office of high priest. In addition, utilization of the call genre provides divine authority for the choice of Joshua to head the priesthood. The prophetic commission, a characteristic formal component of the call, is paralleled in Zechariah 3 by the commission to priestly office. The prophet is typically given a message to impart (Isa 6:9; Jer 1:9-10; Ezek 3:1); this is why the prophet's mouth must be purified (Isa 6:6-7; Jer 1:9). Joshua is not commissioned to deliver a message, but to assume an office. Therefore rather than have his lips purified, he dons pure garments, the sign of that office. It is in the context of Joshua's investiture, therefore, that we must

----

39. See also Long, "Reports," 361.

40. Whether Zech 3:1-7 is in fact drawing on the call genre or whether Zech 3:1-7 and the prophetic calls are drawing on a common genre is a moot point. In the Hebrew Bible as we now have it, Zech 3:1-7 is the only text that presents a commission scene in the divine council in which the primary human participant is not a prophet, but we must allow for the possibility that both priest and king could draw on the <u>topos</u> of a commission in the heavenly assembly without implying that they were thereby laying claim to prophetic authority.

understand the role of the *śāṭān*.

Zech 3:1-7 addresses itself to a terrestrial issue of considerable import, the choice of a high priest to preside over the rejuvenated temple and its cult. From the prophet Ezekiel we learn of the abominations that had polluted the temple prior to the fall of Jerusalem. The temple was full of idols (*gillûlîm*, 8:10), women were weeping for Tammuz (8:14) and men were doing obeisance to the sun (8:16). Although Ezekiel does not specifically mention the priesthood in chapter 8 neither does he exonerate them, and therefore we may assume their tacit approval. Jeremiah explicitly names the priests among those guilty of worshipping "the sun, the moon, and all the host of heaven" (Jer 8:2), and 2 Chr 36:14 informs us that the pre-exilic Jerusalem priesthood followed all the abominations of the nations and thus polluted the temple. If Joshua's immediate forefathers had participated in the apostasy of the old order, should one of their seed indeed be allowed to regain control of temple worship? Although Zech 3:1-7 advocates Joshua's candidacy, we can postulate that certain factions within the restoration community would resist the re-installation of a Zadokite priest.[41] For those Yahwists who had remained in the land and had not been deported to Mesopotamia, the idea of a "foreign" priest presiding over the temple cult may well have been a point of contention. If objections to Joshua's investiture were levelled from within this group, one charge might have been that Joshua had been defiled as a result of living in a foreign land tainted by alien cult

----

41. Indeed, passages such as Isa 66:1 inform us that the very act of rebuilding the temple was controversial.

practises.[42] In short, a variety of reasons can be suggested as potential points of contention within the restoration community with regard to the choice of Joshua as high priest, and thus there is good reason to believe that his proposed investiture met with opposition. The scholars who maintain that Joshua in Zechariah 3 is a cypher for all Israel, therefore, are overlooking evidence that suggests the community itself was divided over the issue of Joshua's suitability for the high priestly office.

Given the highly pragmatic character of Zech 3:1-7, I would propose that the *śāṭān* is depicted as objecting to Joshua's investiture because in fact his assumption of office was not univocally supported within the restoration community. Zech 3:1-7 proclaims that the divine council itself has sanctioned Joshua's appointment as high priest, and presents his exercise of office as a divine commission (v 7). The presence of a celestial *śāṭān* tells us that the objections to his candidacy had been aired even in the heavenly assembly, and had been overruled. With this in mind, let us turn to the interchange between the celestial *śāṭān* and the *malʾāk yhwh*.

Although we can speculate about the nature of the objections raised concerning Joshua's investiture as high priest, the text itself does not delineate the precise charge(s) brought against Joshua in the heavenly court; either the original audience knew them well enough that they did not need to be repeated, or the author is being intentionally vague. All we have is the *malʾāk*

----

42. Nowack, *Die kleinen*, 339; Rudolph, *Sacharja*, 95; Meyers, *Zechariah*, 185, 218.

yhwh's response, and that itself is problematic. The *malʾāk yhwh* counters the unknown charge(s) by saying, *hălôʾ zeh ʾûd muṣāl mēʾēš*, "Is this not a brand rescued from the fire?" Those who would see Joshua as a representative of the entire community typically ground their interpretation in this response of the *malʾāk yhwh*.[43] The fire, they maintain, refers to the exile, and the description "a brand rescued from the fire" is an apt description of the entire community. But as P. Haupt[44] and D. Winton Thomas[45] have noted, *hălôʾ zeh ʾûd muṣāl mēʾēš* is a proverbial expression.[46] Proverbs function to place a problem situation in a recognizable category; they take a personal circumstance and embody it in an impersonal form.[47] They are effective precisely because they can apply to a variety of specific situations, and so although the proverb *could* perhaps be appropriately applied to a group experience, it could equally as well be applied to an individual. The proverb in this case is applied to Joshua, and the issue at hand is investiture. It is intended to counter objections to Joshua becoming high priest. With only this much

----

43. For example, Beuken, *Sacharja*, 283.

44. "The Visions of Zechariah," *JBL* 32 (1913) 119.

45. "Zechariah," 1068.

46. Unlike modern western legal process, it should be noted that proverbs often play a key role in the judiciary procedure of traditional societies. See, for example, John C. Messenger ("The Role of Proverbs in the Nigerian Judicial System," *Southwestern Journal of Anthropology* 15 [1959] 64-73) and Roger D. Abrahams ("Proverbs and Proverbial Expressions," Richard M. Dorson [ed.], *Folklore and Folklife*, 119). Cf. Uriel Simon, "The Poor Man's Ewe-Lamb: An Example of a Juridical Parable," *Biblica* 48 (1967) 207-242.

47. Abrahams, "Proverbs," 119, 121.

information, any attempt to elucidate the referents to which the proverb is applied must be conjectural. Perhaps the mal'āk yhwh is arguing that Joshua's family had survived the conflagration of Jerusalem in 587 B.C.E., and that this should be understood as a sign of divine intervention and favor (see Amos' comments, Amos 4:11, on Sodom and Gomorrah, Gen 19:12-25).[48] The genius of the mal'āk yhwh's response is that it is capable of countering a wide variety of objections, and therein lies its utility. In any event, it need not be understood to apply to the entire community. Context dictates that it refers specifically to Joshua.

In terms of contact with other material in the Hebrew Bible, to my knowledge only one scholar, Nils Johansson,[49] has compared the assembly scene of Zech 3:1-7 to the information available from Job chapters 16 and 33. The mal'āk yhwh of Zechariah 3, like the heavenly mēlîṣ (16:20; 33:23) or mal'āk (33:23) of the book of Job,[50] functions to inform a man of his duty (Job 33:23; Zech 3:7). He is a celestial intermediary who acts both as intercessor and witness.[51] In addition, I would note

----

48. Cf. Meyers, Zechariah, 187.

49. Parakletoi, 35.

50. These passages are discussed in my chapter on the śāṭān in Job.

51. Johansson, Parakletoi, 35. Johansson makes this statement on the basis of wayyāʿad mal'āk yhwh (Zech 3:6), but fails to note that wayyāʿad is construed with the preposition b which, if understood to mean "witness," must mean "witness against" (Boecker, Redeformen, 73). When hʿyd b preceeds a conditional sentence (e.g. Gen 43:3; Exod 19:21; 1 Kgs 2:42), as it does in Zech 3:6, it is better translated "adjure." Thus I prefer to see the witnessing activity in verse 2, and understand verse 6 to introduce the conditions upon which Joshua's access to

that in Job 33:23 the mal'āk announces that he has found a kōper for his human client. In Isa 6:7, the śārāp who purifies Isaiah's lips with a coal taken from the altar says, "this [coal] is now touching your lips; your iniquity [ʿăwōnĕkā] is turned aside and your sin is purified [tĕkuppār].". We have already seen that the changing of Joshua's clothes is the formal equivalent of the purification of Isaiah's lips.[52] Thus, as the mal'āk of Job 33:23 announces that he has found a way to purify his human client, so the mal'āk of Zechariah 3 purifies the high priest Joshua.

The foregoing parallels make it clear that Zechariah 3 partakes of the same conceptual complex as Job 16 and 33. This is significant because in the book of Job, we know that the sufferer's plight is the direct result of the activity of a celestial śāṭān. Although, as we have seen, the passages in Job 16 and 33 that deal with the heavenly intercessor function ironically within the book of Job, we can certainly extrapolate from them the orthodox position on the process of divine law. An individual stands accused by a śāṭān. The case is heard by the heavenly tribunal. For the case to be decided in the accused's favor, a celestial advocate is necessary. These parallels bolster the argument that the heavenly council has convened in Zechariah 3 to hear an individual case pertaining to a particular circumstance.

What, then, of the interpretation that the

----

the divine council rests.

52. It should be noted that the gloss in Zech 3:4 identifies Joshua's change of clothes with the removal of his ʿāwōn, thus tightening the parallel. The gloss also indicates that this early interpreter of the text did not understand Joshua as representing a community; the iniquity is personal.

śāṭān represents the strict process of law in opposition to divine mercy? As I hope I have demonstrated, the issue in Zechariah 3 is not whether the community should be made to continue suffering according to some inflexible law of retributive justice, but whether Joshua should become high priest. Unfortunately, I suspect that underlying the interpretation that the *śāṭān* of Zechariah 3 represents a strict adherence to law that is opposed to divine grace is an anti-Judaic polemic. I would suggest that the *śāṭān* interpreted as the champion of law over grace may present us with a vestige of the medieval notion that equated the devil and the Jew. As Joshua Trachtenberg noted in the preface to his *The Devil and the Jews*,[53] the element in the complex of anti-Jewish prejudice which renders it different, in expression and intensity, from other manifestations of racial or minority antipathy, is the demonological. His book documents the widespread belief in medieval Christendom that the Jews were in league with the devil--indeed, were themselves devils incarnate. Interpreting Zechariah's *śāṭān* as the advocate of strict law over grace is but a more sophisticated and abstract expression of the old equation of the devil and the Jew. Zechariah's *śāṭān* becomes the spokesperson of Jewish law as opposed to Christian grace. The superiority of Christianity is thus affirmed by giving it a textual basis, while Judaism, represented by the *śāṭān*, is pronounced contrary to God's will. Grace supersedes law as the way to community salvation.

----

53. *The Devil and the Jews: The Medieval Conception of the Jew and Its Relation to Modern Anti-Semitism* (New Haven: Yale University, 1943; reprinted Philadelphia: Jewish Publication Society, 1983) xv.

To summarize, we have seen that the interpretation of the *śāṭān*'s role in Zech 3:1-7 has been determined by understanding Joshua to be a cypher for the restoration community. The nature of the vision itself, and especially the fact that it lacks an *angelus interpres*, suggests that Joshua was not intended to to be a symbol for something else. The issue addressed by the vision is Joshua's investiture, which was met with opposition from within the Jerusalem community. The vision informs us that the objections to Joshua's investiture had been heard by the highest possible court, the divine council, and were overruled. Rather than symbolizing the strict adherence to law in opposition to divine mercy, the *śāṭān* of Zech 3:1-7 is the mythological medium through which the author of the passage expresses the conviction that the objections to Joshua's investiture had been voiced in the heavenly court.

Chapter 7

śāṭān IN 1 CHRONICLES 21:1-22:1

Unlike the prologue to Job and Zechariah 3, in 1 Chr 21:1 the noun *śāṭān* appears without the definite article. The major English translations of the Hebrew Bible (KJV, RSV, JB, NEB, etc.) interpret the lack of the definite article to mean that *śāṭān* in 1 Chr 21:1 is being used as a proper name, and the vast majority of modern commentators concur.[1] There have, however, been dissenting voices. Kaupel,[2] Tur-Sinai,[3] and F. X. Kugler[4] have maintained that *śāṭān* in 1 Chr 21:1 is an indefinite noun referring to a human adversary, while T. H. Gaster[5] and Werner Lemke[6] take *śāṭān* to mean an unspecified celestial adversary.[7] The first issue to

----

1. For example, Kurt Galling (*Die Bücher der Chronik, Ezra, Nehemia* [Göttingen: Vandenhoeck und Ruprecht, 1954] 61), Werner Fuss ("2 Samuel 24," *ZAW* 74 [1962] 151), Jacob M. Myers (*1 Chronicles* [AB 12; Garden City: Doubleday, 1965] 145), H. G. M. Williamson (*1 and 2 Chronicles* [Grand Rapids: Eerdmans, 1982] 143) and P. Kyle McCarter (*2 Samuel* [AB 9; Garden City: Doubleday, 1984] 509).

2. *Die Dämonen*, 105-108.

3. *Job*, 44-45.

4. *Von Mose bis Paulus: Forschungen zur Geschichte Israels* (1922) 241-243.

5. "Satan," 225.

6. "Synoptic Studies in the Chronicler's History," unpublished Harvard Ph.D dissertation, 1963, 61 n. 83.

7. Herbert Haag (*Teufelsglaube*, 214 n. 77) notes in passing that the noun *śāṭān* in 1 Chr 21:1 may be

tackle, therefore, is whether *śāṭān* in 1 Chr 21:1 should be understood as an indefinite common noun or a proper name.

If we set aside for the moment 1 Chronicles 21, the earliest datable evidence for *śāṭān* used as a proper name comes from *Jub*. 23:29 and *As*. *Mos*. 10:1, both of which can be dated to the persecutions of Antiochus IV ca. 168 B.C.E..[8] The deuterocanonical texts that antedate 168 B.C.E. speak of evil demons and corrupt angels, but no text uses the name Satan. In Tobit, for instance, the evil demon who had to be restrained before Tobit could marry Sarah is named Asmodeus (Tob 3:8, 17). In the earliest level of *1 Enoch* 6-11, the leader of the angels who were punished as a consequence of their intercourse with the daughters of men is Shemihazah; in a later addition to these chapters, he is called Asael.[9] In short, whereas the deuterocanonical literature prior to 168 B.C.E. speaks of specific names for evil demons

----

indefinite, but develops his treatment of the passage with the understanding that it is a proper name.

8. For the dating of these references, see George Nickelsburg (*Jewish Literature Between the Bible and the Mishnah* [Philadelphia: Fortress, 1981] 78, 80-83, 96 n. 18). Probably stemming from the same decade are the references to a Satan in *Jub*. 10:11, 40:9, 46:2 and 50:5 (Nickelsburg, *Jewish Literature*, 79). In Sir 21:27 we have *ton satanan*; this could mean that the Hebrew *Vorlage* was *haśśāṭān* and therefore a common noun, but because it is possible in Greek to construe a proper name with the definite article, it is conceivable that the Hebrew *Vorlage* was *śāṭān*, used as a proper name. If so, the earliest datable use of *śāṭān* as a proper name would be ca. 180 B.C.E..

9. For the identification of primary and secondary strata in *1 Enoch* 6-11, see Nickelsburg (*Jewish Literature*, 49-50, 52) and Paul Hanson ("Rebellion in Heaven, Azazel, and Euhemeristic Heroes in 1 Enoch 6-11," *JBL* 96 [1977] 197). Hanson ("Rebellion," 197) dates the primary stratum to the third century B.C.E..

and corrupt angels, no extant tradition employs the proper name Satan.[10] The available evidence, therefore, points to the second century B.C.E. for the earliest occurences of the proper name Satan.

There is at present no consensus among scholars concerning the dating of the books of Chronicles. Prior to the 1960s, mainline scholarship viewed Chronicles as an integral part of a composition extending through the books of Ezra and Nehemiah, and consequently dated Chronicles no earlier than the third quarter of the fifth

----

10. Even contemporary with and subsequent to the persecutions of Antiochus Epiphanes, Satan was neither the exclusive nor the most popular name for a celestial power of evil. In retelling the sacrifice of Isaac, _Jub_. 17:16 informs us that it was prince Mastema who suggested that Abraham's piety required testing. According to the same source, it was also prince Mastema who attacked Moses on his return to Egypt (_Jub_. 48:2). At Qumran, the leader of the forces of darkness was named Belial (Yigael Yadin, _The Scroll of the War of the Sons of Light Against the Sons of Darkness_, [Oxford: Oxford University, 1962] 232). The word _śāṭān_ occurs three times at Qumran (1QH 4:6 _bkl śṭn mšḥyt_; 45:3 _kl śṭn wmšḥyt_; 1QSb 1:8 _[k]l śṭn_); in no instance is it clearly a proper name. (So also Gaster, "Satan," 225.) In the parables of Enoch (_1 Enoch_ 37-71, dating from the Herodian period), _satanas_ is pluralized. _1 Enoch_ 40:7 tells us that the fourth archangel (Phanuel) had the task of fending off the satans (Satans ?) and forbidding them to accuse human beings before God. As late as the Herodian period, therefore, we have evidence for a plurality of heavenly accusers.

When we turn to the Septuagint translation of 1 Chr 21:1, we learn that _śāṭān_ is translated by the Greek common noun _diabolos_ (Edwin Hatch and Henry Redpath, _A Concordance to the Septuagint_ [Graz: Akademische Druck-U. Verlagsanstalt, 1954] vol. 1, 299). If the translator had understood _śāṭān_ to be a proper name, he would have simply transliterated the Hebrew. We must infer, therefore, that the translator understood _śāṭān_ to be a common noun.

century B.C.E..[11] In 1961 David Noel Freedman[12] challenged this position, detaching the books of Chronicles from Ezra-Nehemiah and arguing that the books of Chronicles were written to establish and defend the claims of the house of David within the context of the early restoration community, the same community addressed by the prophets Haggai and Zechariah ca. 515 B.C.E..[13] Stylistic and linguistic evidence arguing against the common authorship of Chronicles and Ezra-Nehemiah was provided in 1968 by Sara Japhet,[14] thus strengthening Freedman's contention that the dating of Chronicles need not be tied to the dating of Ezra and Nehemiah. In 1975, John Newsome[15] and Frank Moore Cross[16] published articles in support of Freedman's position. Cross refined the argument by identifying three levels in the compilation process of Chronicles-Ezra-Nehemiah, the

----

11. For discussion and references, see James D. Newsome ("Toward a New Understanding of the Chronicler and his Purposes," JBL 94 [1975] 201-202). The most commonly accepted date was ca. 400 B.C.E.. Cf. Steven McKenzie, The Chronicler's Use of the Deuteronomistic History (HSM 33; Atlanta: Scholars, 1985) 17-32.

12. "The Chronicler's Purpose," CBQ 23 (1961) 436-442.

13. Freedman, "Purpose," 440-441.

14. "The Supposed Common Authorship of Chronicles and Ezra-Nehemiah Investigated Anew," VT 18 (1968) 330-371. Note that Japhet's orthographic data has been challenged by Cross ("Reconstruction," 14 n. 58). Cf. Mark Throntveit, "Linguistic Analysis and the Question of Authorship in Chronicles, Ezra, and Nehemiah," VT 32 (1982) 203.

15. "New Understanding," 201-217.

16. "Reconstruction," 12-14.

earliest of which[17] he dated to the founding of the Second Temple, ca.520 B.C.E..

Whereas Freedman's analysis (and Cross' refinement thereof) has not been universally accepted *in toto*, scholarship since 1961 has been increasingly inclined to view 1 Chr 10-2 Chr 34[18] as thematically and chronologically distinct from Ezra-Nehemiah.[19] The final redaction of Chronicles-Ezra-Nehemiah is best dated ca. 400 B.C.E.[20] and, if Freedman and Cross are correct, the earliest literary stratum, which would include 1 Chr 21:1-22:1, is a product of the restoration community ca. 520 B.C.E.. If we combine these findings with our discussion of deuterocanonical literature, we are faced with a gap of approximately 230 years between the final redaction of Chronicles-Ezra-Nehemiah and the first clear mention of Satan. And if Cross is correct in

----

17. 1 Chr 10-2 Chr 34 plus the *Vorlage* of 1 Esdr 1:1-5:65 (=2 Chr 34:1-Ezra 3:13). Cf. Cross, "Reconstruction," 13. Cross dubbed this level Chr^1.

18. The genealogical section (1 Chr 1-9) does not derive from the same source.

19. In addition to Japhet (cited above), see for example H. G. M. Williamson (*Israel in the Books of Chronicles* [Cambridge: Cambridge University, 1977]; *1 and 2 Chronicles* [Grand Rapids: Eerdmans, 1982] esp. 9-17) and R. Braun ("Chronicles, Ezra and Nehemiah: Theology and Literary History," J. A. Emerton [ed.], *Studies in the Historical Books of the Old Testament* [VTSup 30; Leiden: Brill, 1979] 52-64). John Newsome ("New Understanding"), Steven McKenzie (*Chronicler's Use*, 25-26) and D. L. Petersen (*Late Israelite Prophecy: Studies in the Deutero-Prophetic Literature and in Chronicles* [Missoula: Scholars, 1977] 57-60) accept not only the separation of 1 Chr 10-2 Chr 34 from Ezra-Nehemiah, but also the sixth century date.

20. Cross, "Reconstruction," 11-18; McKenzie, *Chronicler's Use*, 24, 30-31, n. 32.

assigning Chr[1] to the late sixth century, the gap becomes a veritable chasm. I conclude therefore that there is no *prima-facie* evidence to suggest that *śāṭān* in 1 Chr21:1 is being used as a proper name. With this in mind, let us turn to our passage.

1 Chr 21:1-22:1 is paralleled in the Deuteronomistic history by 2 Samuel 24. Both passages tell the story of a census taken during the reign of David, an ensuing plague, and an altar built on the threshing floor of Araunah (2 Sam 24) / Ornan (1 Chr 21). In 2 Sam 24:1 the story begins, "and the anger of Yahweh again burned against Israel, and he provoked David against them, saying 'Go number Israel and Judah.'" David did as Yahweh instructed him, and in response, Yahweh brought a plague (v 15).[21] The introductory verse links chapter 24 with 2 Samuel 21,[22] which tells of another natural disaster during the reign of David, namely a three year famine.

----

21. The story as it now stands in 2 Samuel is a composite narrative. Although 24:1 makes it clear that Yahweh was the ultimate cause of the census and ensuing plague, verses 10 and 17 lay the blame on David. In verse 16 we are told that Yahweh, unprompted, halts the plague at the threshing floor of Araunah, yet verse 25 maintains that it was not until David built an altar and propitiated the deity that Yahweh was persuaded to halt the plague. From these and other discrepancies (cf. McCarter, *2 Samuel*, 514) it is clear that the narrative of 2 Samuel 24 is composite, although the precise division into contributing sources is disputed. Cf. McCarter, *2 Samuel*, 514-516; Werner Fuss, "2 Samuel 24," *ZAW* 74 (1962) 149-160. For the relationship between census and plague, see J. R. Kupper ("Le recensement dans les textes de Mari," A. Parrot [ed.], *Studia Mariana* [Leiden: Brill, 1950] 99-110), E. A. Speiser ("Census and Ritual Expiation in Mari and Israel," *BASOR* 149 [1958] 17-25), and McCarter (*2 Samuel*, 512-514).

22. Cf. McCarter, *2 Samuel*, 509.

2 Samuel 21 attributes this famine to bloodguilt incurred by Saul's treatment of the Gibeonites, and thus the two chapters taken together originally functioned as an apologetic, exonerating David from any blame for the respective catastrophes.

The Chronicler included the census plague story in his history of the reign of David because he understood the altar built by David in response to the plague to be the altar of the Solomonic temple (1 Chr 22:1). The Chronicler was highly selective in terms of the material he chose to transmit concerning the reign of David. On the one hand, he generally deleted material (such as the Bathsheba incident, Nathan's rebuke, and the revolt of Absalom) counterproductive to his goal of demonstrating that David was an ideal monarch. On the other hand, he rearranged the order of his source material, for instance to give the impression that David's first act after securing Jerusalem was to attend to the ark.[23] The Chronicler had three primary objectives in his treatment of the reign of David: to show that David was the legitimate king for all Israel,[24] to smooth over any reference to internal opposition (e.g. Bathsheeba, Nathan, Absalom; see above), and to portray David as the founder and organizer

----

23. McKenzie, Chronicler's Use, 41.

24. Note, for instance, that 1 Chronicles 11 portrays all Israel accepting David's kingship at Hebron, whereas 2 Sam 2:4 informs us that David was initially anointed by the men of Judah, and only later accepted as king by Israel (2 Sam 5:1-3; cf. Williamson, Israel, 96-96). If we place this pan-Israel Tendenz within the context of the early restoration period, we can posit that the Chronicler was encouraging the remnant of the northern tribes to support the Jerusalemite program for a rejuvenated monarchy and cult (McKenzie, Chronicler's Use, 74-75).

of Israel's cultic life (1 Chr 23-27). It was for the third reason that the Chronicler included the story of the census, plague, and altar building.

As mentioned above, the story of the census in 2 Samuel 24 begins, "and the anger of Yahweh _again_ [my emphasis] burned against Israel." Although a precedent for Yahweh's anger was supplied in the Deuteronomistic history by the three year famine of 2 Samuel 21, this precedent was not included in the Chronicler's history. Thus the introduction to the census plague story that the Chronicler found in the Deuteronomistic history was unsuitable, and provided good reason for the Chronicler to alter his source.[25] 1 Chr 21:1 reads, "and a _śāṭān_ stood up against Israel, and provoked David to number Israel."[26] Why did the Chronicler choose this locution, and what does it imply?

The most prevalent explanation is that the Chronicler was striving to clean up Yahweh's image.[27]

----

25. Rudolf Mosis, _Untersuchungen zur Theologie des chronistischen Geschichteswerkes_ (Freiburg: Herder, 1973) 112 and n. 91. Note that the Chronicler rewrote introductions to other stories when his source proved inappropriate, for instance 2 Chr 18:1-3 (replacing 1 Kgs 22:1-3).

26. Note the substitution of "Israel" for 2 Sam 24:1's "Israel and Judah." This is another example of the Chronicler's pan-Israel interest, and thus is a good indication that the Chronicler composed 1 Chr 21:1.

27. For example, Duhm (_Die bösen Geister_, 61), von Rad ("_diabolos_," 74, and _Das Geschichtsbild des chronistischen Werkes_ [Stuttgart: W. Kohlhammer, 1930] 8), Kluger (_Satan_, 155, 159), Haag (_Teufelsglaube_, 207, 213), J. W. Rothstein and D. J. Hänel (_Kommentar zum ersten Buch der Chronik_ [KAT 18; Leipzig: Scholl, 1927] 379, 384), Rudolph Kittel (_Der Bücher der Chronik_ [HAT 6; Göttingen: Vandenhoeck und Ruprecht, 1902] 80), Kurt Galling (_Die Bücher der Chronik, Ezra, Nehemia_

Kluger,[28] for instance, describes this in terms of cleansing Yahweh of his dark side; Haag[29] expresses the claim theologically, stating that the Chronicler removes Yahweh from any causal relationship to sin. I maintain that this position is too general, and reads too much into the text. The appeal to a growing concern in the books of Chronicles for ridding Yahweh of malevolent behavior as a motive for rewriting 1 Chr 21:1 predates the recognition that the themes of 1 Chr 10-2 Chr 34 are not the same as the themes of Ezra-Nehemiah. Since that recognition has been made, concern for Yahweh's purity has not been identified and discussed as a major theme of the Chronicler. Furthermore, if one wanted to maintain that the Chronicler was concerned with cleaning up Yahweh's image, how could one explain the episode of Micaiah ben Imlah, for instance, in which the Chronicler was content to retain the description of Yahweh sanctioning the spirit's proposal to become a lying spirit in the mouths of Ahab's prophets, thus luring Ahab into defeat at Ramoth-Gilead (2 Chr 18:18-22)? Or, to take another example, why would the Chronicler relate that Yahweh was responsible for causing Rehoboam to ignore the advice of his seasoned counselors and thereby forfeit the northern kingdom (2 Chr 10:15)? If the Chronicler rewrote 2 Sam 24:1 in order to remove Yahweh from any causal relationship to sin, why were these other incidents transmitted without emendation? These two examples make it plain that the Chronicler had no qualms about portraying Yahweh as the instigator of actions designed to cause harm, nor was he loathe to admit that

----

[Göttingen: Vandenhoeck und Ruprecht, 1954] 61), and McKenzie (Chronicler's Use, 67).

28. Satan, 159.

29. Teufelsglaube, 207.

Yahweh would use as a vehicle a _rûaḥ šeqer_, "lying spirit." In short, I do not think that the Chronicler rewrote 1 Chr 21:1 because his vision of deity was significantly more pure than that of his predecessors. Rather, I would look more closely at the context of 1 Chr 21:1.

As mentioned above, the Chronicler presents an idealized portrait David's reign. For this reason, he omitted material such as the Bathsheba incident and Nathan's rebuke. He was obliged to include the story of the census plague because it culminated in the erection of what he understood to be the altar of the Solomonic temple. I would postulate, therefore, that the Chronicler's objection to his received text was not that Yahweh incited an action that led to divine punishment, but that Yahweh was said to be unaccountably angry with Israel _during the reign of the idealized monarch David_, and that Yahweh therefore provoked _David_ to commit a punishable offense.[30] Not only does the Chronicler wish to downplay Yahweh's complicity, he also interprets the census account in a way that at least partially shifts the blame from David to Joab. This shift of blame can be demonstrated by comparing 2 Samuel 24 with 1 Chronicles 21 and 27. In 2 Sam 24:9 we are told that Joab completed the census, and immediately thereafter (v 10) David admits that he has committed a sin. 1 Chronicles 21, on the other hand, relates a different story. In 1 Chr 21:6 we are told that Joab did not include Levi and Benjamin in his total,[31] and this

----

30. Von Rad ("_diabolos_," 74-75) has also made this point.

31. This detail has occasioned much comment. It is generally claimed that the Chronicler excludes Levi in order to comply with the prohibition against counting

statement is immediately followed (v 7) not by David's confession of sin, but by the comment that "this thing was evil in the eyes of God, and he smote Israel." That "this thing" was understood to refer to Joab's omission of Levi and Benjamin and not David's original command to number the people is made explicit in the reference to David's census in 1 Chr 27:24a: "Joab ben Zeruiah began to number, but he did not finish, and it was because of this that wrath came upon Israel." Clearly, then, the Chronicler is interpreting his source in a way that shifts blame away from David. I am suggesting that 1 Chr 21:1 indicates that Yahweh's complicity was also being downplayed, because the relationship between Yahweh and *this king in particular* was of paramount concern to the Chronicler.

The assertion that 1 Chr 21:1 demonstrates an effort to rid Yahweh of malevolent behavior is often coupled with the claim that the deity of the Chronicler is a transcendent deity.[32] This claim, again generated when scholarship did not differentiate between the themes of the Chronicler and those of Ezra-Nehemiah, is in need of a general review and re-evaluation. For our limited purposes, I note that the appeal to Yahweh's transcendence typically has been made on the basis that

---

Levi in Num 1:47-49 and 2:33 (for example, Rothstein, *Chronik*, 365). The reason for excluding Benjamin is less agreed upon, although the most popular explanation is that the tabernacle was residing within Benjamin's borders (Rothstein, *Chronik*, 366). In light of the impact that 4QSam[a] has had upon Chronicles research, I would caution against attributing the mention of Levi and Benjamin to the Chronicler's *Tendenz*, especially in this case because Levi and Benjamin are mentioned in Josephus' account of 2 Samuel 24 (*Jewish Antiquities*, book 7, line 319).

32. For example, Rothstein (*Chronik*, 380) and von Rad (*Geschichtsbild*, 9-10).

the Chronicler presents us with a more developed angelology;[33] Yahweh has retreated to a higher heaven, and his will is carried out through divine intermediaries.[34] The prooftext for positing a more developed angelology in the books of Chronicles is 1 Chronicles 21, the chapter currently under investigation. In order to demonstrate a more developed angelology, scholars have compared the extent of the role played by the malʾāk yhwh in 1 Chronicles 21 with the parallel account in 2 Samuel 24. In order to evaluate this claim, let us turn to the relevant texts. First, the MT of 2 Samuel 24:

> [15]And Yahweh imposed a plague on Israel, from the morning until an appointed time, and 70,000 men died from amongst the people, from Dan to Beersheba. [16]And the malʾāk sent forth his hand against Jerusalem to destroy it, and Yahweh repented of the evil, and he said to the malʾāk who was causing destruction amongst the people, "It is enough; stay your hand." Now the malʾāk yhwh was by the threshing floor of Araunah the Jebusite. [17]And David spoke to Yahweh when he saw the malʾāk who was smiting the people, and he said, "I have sinned and committed iniquity, but these are sheep: what have they done? Put forth your hand against me and my father's house."

In 1 Chronicles 21, the malʾāk yhwh is introduced earlier in the narrative, in the first speech

----

33. For example, H. Schmid ("Der Templebau Solomos in religiongeschichtlicher Sicht," A. Kuschke [ed.], Archäologie und Altes Testament [Tübingen: J.C.B. Mohr, 1970] 246), Kittel (Chronik, 80) and Rothstein (Chronik, 381).

34. Rothstein, Chronik, 380.

of Gad (21:12; *malʾāk yhwh mašḥît bĕkol-gĕbûl yiśrāʾēl*). Corresponding to 2 Sam 24:15-17, the Chronicler offers the following description:

> 14 And Yahweh imposed a plague on Israel, and there
> fell from Israel 70,000 men. 15 And God sent forth
> a *malʾāk* against Jerusalem to destroy it, but when
> Yahweh saw the destruction he repented of the evil,
> and said to the destroying *malʾāk*, "It is enough;
> stay your hand.". Now the *malʾāk yhwh* was standing
> by the threshing floor of Ornan the Jebusite.
> 16 And David lifted up his eyes and saw the *malʾāk*
> *yhwh* standing between the earth and the heavens,
> and his sword was drawn in his hand, outstretched
> against Jerusalem. And David and the elders,
> clothed in sackcloth, fell down on their faces.
> 17 And David said to God, "Did I not order to count
> the people? And it is I who have sinned and indeed
> done wrong. But these are sheep, what have they
> done? O Yahweh my God, put forth your hand against
> me and against the house of my father, but against
> your people let there be no plague."

In the following verse the *malʾāk yhwh* instructs Gad to speak to David, and in verse 20 Ornan sees the *malʾāk*. After David builds the altar and offers the appropriate sacrifices, Yahweh commands the *malʾāk* to put his sword back in its sheath (v 27). In the Chronicler's addition to the story (21:28-22:1) we are told that David did not inquire of the Lord at Gibeon because he was afraid of the sword of the *malʾāk yhwh*.[35]

----

35. On this point, see Paul E. Dion ("The Angel with the Drawn Sword [2 [sic] Chr 21,16]: An Exercise in Restoring the Balance of Text Criticism *and* Attention to Context," *ZAW* 97 [1985] 114-117).

The above synopsis of 2 Samuel 24 and 1 Chronicles 21 certainly indicates that the *malʾāk yhwh* plays a larger role in the latter text. However, comparison of these texts with 4QSam[a] provides evidence that the discrepancies between MT 2 Samuel 24 and 1 Chronicles 21 are not a result of differing conceptual worlds emanating from different historical periods but rather result from differing textual traditions.[36] The portion of 4QSam[a] that corresponds to 2 Sam 24:16 reads:[37]

> And [David] lifted up [his eyes and he saw the *malʾāk yhwh* standing between] the earth and the heavens, and his swor[d] was drawn in his hand, [outstretched against Jerusalem, and David and the elders fell on] their [fac]es, clo[thed] in sackcloth.

Eugene Ulrich[38] and Steven McKenzie[39] have demonstrated that 4QSam[a] is not dependent on 1 Chr 21:16 for this reading. Unfortunately, 2 Samuel 24 is not extant in its entirety in 4QSam[a], but the above excerpt

----

36. 4QSam[a] is an exemplar of the Palestinian text type that served as the *Vorlage* of 1 Chronicles. When 4QSam[a] agrees with MT 1 Chr against MT Sam, it is highly probable that the Chronicler was simply following his *Vorlage*. Cf. McKenzie, *Chronicler's Use*, 26-27.

37. For the text, see Eugene Ulrich (*The Qumran Text of Samuel and Josephus* [HSM 19; Missoula: Scholars, 1978] 156-157) or Steven McKenzie (*Chronicler's Use*, 55). Cf. Werner Lemke, "The Synoptic Problem in the Chronicler's History," *HTR* 58 (1965) 355-356.

38. *Qumran*, 157. Cf. F. M. Cross, *The Ancient Library of Qumran and Modern Biblical Studies* (Garden City: Doubleday, 1961) 188 n. 40a; Lemke, "Synoptic Studies," 70.

39. *Chronicler's Use*, 56.

makes it possible to argue that the Chronicler did not create a more extensive role for the mal'āk yhwh. Rather, he was simply following his text of 2 Samuel.[40] Furthermore, it can be remarked that the first mention of the mal'āk in 2 Samuel 24, at verse 16, reads simply hammal'āk, which suggests that at some point in the textual tradition of 2 Samuel 24, the messenger had been introduced prior to verse 16. Thus not only does 1 Chronicles 21 preserve a different textual tradition, it preserves a superior textual tradition. Finally, it should be noted that 4QSam[a] describes the mal'āk yhwh poised in mid-air, "[standing between] the earth and the heavens." The specific fact that the messenger of 1 Chr 21:16 is described as hovering in mid-air (as opposed to standing on the ground) has been widely used to support the contention that the Chronicler had an advanced notion of angels.[41] 4QSam[a] proves this contention clearly fallacious. Thus I see no reason to believe that the Chronicler substituted śāṭān for Yahweh because he conceived of a more extensive or more developed role for divine intermediaries.

To sum up our findings thus far, we have seen that there is no evidence to support reading śāṭān as a proper name in Chronicles. Recent research into the composition of Chronicles-Ezra-Nehemiah suggests a redactional history which would date 1 Chr 21:1-22:1 between 520 and 400 B.C.E., yet the earliest clear

----

40. McKenzie (Chronicler's Use, 56-57) argues convincingly that the mention of the mal'āk in verse 18 is an expansion, although not a tendentious one, and that the reference to the mal'āk in verse 20 is the result of textual corruption.

41. For example, Kittel (Chronik, 80); Rothstein (Chronik, 382).

evidence for understanding śāṭān as a proper name comes from the second century. The reasons most commonly posited to account for the Chronicler's turn of phrase in 1 Chr 21:1 (i.e. cleaning up Yahweh's image and/or an appeal to Yahweh's transcendence) need to be re-evaluated in light of the recognition that 1 Chr 10-2 Chr 34 is thematically and chronologically independent of Ezra-Nehemiah. What we do know is that the Chronicler's account of the reign of David was designed to portray David as an ideal ruler, a king for all Israel and the founder and organizer of Israel's cultic life. In 2 Samuel 24, the story of the census plague was introduced in a way that alluded to a three year famine earlier in David's reign. The Chronicler did not include the famine account in his history, and thus his source's introduction was inappropriate, and invited change. Rather than credit Yahweh with provoking David to commit an act that would cause his people harm, the Chronicler downplayed Yahweh's complicity by introducing the common noun śāṭān in place of Yahweh. He likewise attempted to shift blame from David by crediting God's anger to the fact that Joab did not complete the census.

If the term śāṭān is not being used as a proper name in 1 Chr 21:1, how should it be understood? As mentioned at the beginning of this chapter, those scholars who have translated śāṭān in 1 Chr 21:1 as an indefinite common noun are divided over whether the term refers to a human adversary or a celestial one. I shall examine each of these possibilities in turn.

As we saw in chapter 3, the noun śāṭān is used to refer to terrestrial adversaries of the Israelite state (1 Kgs 11:14, 23-24). 1 Chr 21:1 tells us that a śāṭān "stood up against" (converted imperfect of ʿāmad plus ʿal) Israel, thus provoking David to take a census of the people. This census, it should be noted, was carried out by military officers (v 2) and the report brought back to David informed him only of the number of able-bodied fighting men (v 5). In 2 Chr 20:23 *ʿāmad* plus *ʿal* is used to describe the Ammonites' and Moabites' act of rising in battle against the inhabitants of Seir, thus demonstrating that the Chronicler was familiar with the expression *ʿāmad ʿal* in the context of military aggression. A case can be made, therefore, for understanding the *śāṭān* who arose against Israel and provoked David to take a census for military purposes to be an unspecified human enemy of the Israelite state.

The alternative to understanding the Chronicler's *śāṭān* to be a human military adversary is to understand the term as referring to an unspecified member of the celestial assembly.[42] Understood in this manner, this celestial *śāṭān* could be construed either 1) as an unnamed adversary who, like the *rûaḥ šeqer* of 1 Kings 22 who proposed to the divine assembly[43] a plan whereby Ahab could be lured to his death, rises up against Israel and provokes David to take a census, or 2) as a divine accuser who brings an unspecified charge[44] against

----

42. Tur-Sinai (*Job*, 43-44) suggested a third possibility, viz. that the *śāṭān* of 1 Chronicles 21 is a false prophet acting as *agent provocateur*. The context offers no clue as to why an unnamed false prophet would be alluded to at this point in the story.

43. Although the divine assembly context is not certain in 1 Chr 21:1, it is possible that the verb *ʿāmad*, a verb used as a technical term for participation in the divine council (Cross, "Council of Yahweh," 274 n.3), indicates that we should infer a council setting.

44. Note that no charge is explicit in Zechariah 3, a text which clearly envisages a divine council context, nor does the Chronicler's sourcetext (2 Samuel 24) provide a reason for Yahweh's ire.

Israel to the heavenly assize.[45] Given the extreme terseness of 1 Chr 21:1 it is difficult to choose between these two possibilities. In either event the substitution of *śāṭān* for the wrath of Yahweh serves to distance Yahweh from the subsequent act of instigating David to take a census. In that the announcement of divine wrath is itself a legalistic expression,[46] understanding *śāṭān* to mean "an accuser" has the dual advantage of remaining faithful to the contextual sense of the sourcetext while at the same time completely obscuring the identity of said celestial accuser. Thus I prefer to understand the Chronicler's *śāṭān* as a divine accuser rather than either a terrestrial or celestial adversary.

Finally, mention should be made once again of Num 22:22-35. In this passage, Yahweh's anger leads to the dispatch of a sword-wielding messenger who confronts Balaam on his way to meet the king of Moab. As we have seen above, this is precisely parallel what was described in the Chronicler's source; Yahweh's anger burned against

----

45. As we have seen, in Job 1-2 and Zechariah 3 the noun *śaṭān* is very much at home in a celestial legal context. 1 Chr 21:1's *ʿāmad ʿal*, in addition to its use in the military sphere (see above) is commonly used in the legal arena as a term expressing opposition (Judg 6:31; 2 Chr 26:18; Ezra 10:15). Von Rad ("*diabolos*," 74) also notes the legal connotation of *ʿāmad ʿal*.

46. Dennis McCarthy, "The Wrath of Yahweh and the Structural Unity of the Deuteronomistic History," J. L. Crenshaw and J. T. Willis (eds.), *Essays in Old Testament Ethics* (New York: Ktav, 1974) 100. Catastrophes such as war, pestilence, or famine could be described as ensuing either due to Yahweh's wrath, as in the plague of 2 Samuel 24, or as a result of divine judgment, as for example in Ezek 14:21. Thus the Chronicler's *wayyaʿămōd śāṭān ʿal-yiśrāʾēl* would not differ conceptually from (*wayyōsep*) *ʾap-yhwh laḥărôt bĕyiśrāʾēl* (2 Sam 24:1a).

Israel, and so the sword-wielding mal'āk yhwh was sent forth to smite the object of divine wrath. In Num 22:22, God dispatches the sword-wielding messenger lĕśāṭān. In 1 Chr 21:1 we have the same sword-wielding messenger, the mal'āk yhwh, who is the vehicle through which divine displeasure is expressed. Implicitly, then, the mal'āk yhwh of 1 Chronicles 21 has also been dispatched lĕśāṭān. In effect, 1 Chronicles 21 speaks of two celestial satans; the first is an unspecified accuser who brings a complaint against Israel to the heavenly tribunal, and the second is the messenger dispatched as a consequence of Yahweh's wrath.

CONCLUSIONS

The noun *śāṭān* is used with two, and possibly three, distinct meanings in the Hebrew Bible. The first is "adversary," and this meaning is evidenced in both the terrestrial (1 Sam 29; 1 Kgs 5, 11) and celestial (Num 22) spheres. The second meaning, "accuser," describes a role that could be assumed by someone with a legal complaint. Again, the term could have a human (2 Sam 19; Ps 109) or a divine (1 Chr 21) referent. In two contexts, both of which are set in the heavenly assize (Job 1-2; Zech 3), the noun *śāṭān* may designate a post or office of accuser, but this meaning cannot be confirmed by comparison with ancient Near Eastern terrestrial or mythological court models, nor can it be demonstrated that only one office of divine accuser was envisaged. In any event, there is no single celestial *śāṭān*.

The *śāṭān* of Numbers 22 is the *malʾāk yhwh*, who was dispatched because Balaam piqued divine anger by embarking on a journey against Yahweh's will. The story of Balaam and the ass does not derive from epic tradition. Indeed, epic tradition portrays Balaam as a model intermediary, while the Balaam of Numbers 22:22-34 is clearly being ridiculed for his inability to perceive the divine. In the tradition preserved at Deir ʿAllā, the abnormal behavior of animals is a central feature. The Balaam of Deir ʿAllā reports this atypical behavior to his people in the context of transmitting the gods' intentions to precipitate a cosmic cataclysm. The Balaam of Num 22:22-34 cannot even perceive the implications in his own life of an animal well-known to him acting in a thoroughly antithetical fashion. The disparity between the Balaam of epic tradition and the Balaam of Num 22:22-34, combined with an analysis of Balaam traditions found outside the Balaam cycle and with the conclusions reached by scholars who recently have studied the Balaam cycle, suggest that the ass story should be dated no earlier than the second half of the sixth century B.C.E.. This means that the malʾāk yhwh as śāṭān cannot be relegated to the murky prehistory of a single śāṭān figure. The sword-wielding malʾāk of Numbers 22 can be compared with his counterpart in 1 Chronicles 21, and the implication drawn that 1 Chronicles 21 in effect mentions not one, but two, celestial satans.

The Joban śāṭān accuses Yahweh of perpetrating a world order in which piety is not tested; if the righteous inevitably prosper, how can one be sure that they are not motivated by base greed? Within the context of the folktale prologue, normal world order is rescinded, and a man tām wĕyāšār is made to suffer. Ironically, Job attributes his suffering to the fact that God hedges him in (3:23), whereas the audience knows that Job's misfortunes have been brought about for precisely the opposite reason (1:10). Although the link between piety and reward is initially severed in the make-believe world of the folktale, this proposition also underlies the "real" world of the dialogue cycle. The audience knows this, but the characters of the dialogue do not. The disparity between what the audience knows to be true and what the characters in the dialogue affirm creates the potential for irony. One of the ways in which this irony is manifested revolves around Job's plea for a divine intermediary who could lay his hand on both God and man (9:33), who would witness for him in the heavenly tribunal (16:19-21) and thus rescue him from death

(19:25; cf. 33:23-25). What Job does not realize is that his condition is the result of a divine intermediary who has affected both himself and God, and whose testimony has propelled Job toward the grave rather than saving him from it. The audience, privy to the prologue, was well aware of the *śāṭān*'s actions, and thus, ironically, Job's heavenly witness is in fact the *śāṭān*. No heavenly intercessor effects the restoration of Job's fortunes; rather, Job is forced to accept deity in its cosmic aspect, bending his knee to the God who describes to him an amoral universe, thus proving the accuser wrong. Individual justice becomes the storybook ending, and with it the death-knell is sounded for the religion of the personal god.

The *śāṭān* of Zechariah 3 is also a celestial accuser. The passage in which he appears, Zech 3:1-7, is a later addition to a cycle of seven visions originally constructed to highlight Zechariah's vision of diarchy. Because Zech 3:1-7 is stylistically independent of the other seven visions, it is incorrect to view Joshua the high priest as a cypher for the restoration community. Rather, Joshua's investiture was met with opposition from within that community, although the precise charges levelled by Joshua's detractors are not explicit. The *śāṭān*, therefore, does not represent a strict adherence to retributive justice that is opposed to divine mercy, but rather is the mythological medium through which the community is told that the objections to Joshua's investiture had been voiced in the highest possible court, the divine council, and were overruled.

1 Chr 21:1 does not use *śāṭān* as a proper name, but rather employs it as an indefinite common noun referring to an unspecified member of the heavenly assembly. Recent scholarship on the redactional history

of Chronicles-Ezra-Nehemiah places the earliest stratum of the work, Chr^{1}, in the fourth quarter of the sixth century B.C.E., whereas the earliest references to a Satan stem from the second century B.C.E.. 1 Chr 21:1-22:1 is paralleled in the Deuteronomistic history by 2 Samuel 24. The latter passage begins, "and the anger of Yahweh again burned against Israel, and he provoked David to number them.". This introductory verse linked 2 Samuel 24 to 2 Samuel 21, which tells of a famine that occurred as a result of bloodguilt incurred by Saul's treatment of the Gibeonites. The Chronicler did not transmit the story of the famine, and hence 2 Sam 24:1 was not a suitable introduction to the Chronicler's rendition of the census plague. Because the Chronicler wished to portray the reign of David as paradigmatic, the relationship between Yahweh and *this king in particular* was of paramount importance. Thus the Chronicler shifted the blame for the census plague from David to Joab, and also downplayed Yahweh's complicity. Instead of Yahweh prompting David to sin, the Chronicler foists responsibility upon an unnamed celestial accuser.

APPENDIX

BEELZEBUL, BEELZEBUB, AND *bĕʿēl dĕbābāʾ*

One of the questions posed, but not satisfactorily answered, by modern scholarship is why *Beelzeboul* came to be used as a name for Satan (Matt 10:25;12:24,27; Mark 3:22; Luke 11:15,18,19). Three main proposals have been offered, all of which are based primarily on a semantic analysis of the name Beelzebul, or the variant Beelzebub.[1] The first proposal takes as its starting point Matt 10:25, and posits that this verse intentionally etymologizes the name Beelzebul by identifying its bearer as the "master [*bʿl*] of the house [*zbl*]."[2] The second proposal posits that Greek -*zeboul* reflects Aramaic -*zîbbûl*, "dung," and as such is a cacophemistic substitution, perhaps for -*zîbbûaḥ*, "sacrifice."[3] The third and least popular proposition

----

1. The element -*zeboul* is supported by all the Greek manuscripts, and must be considered the superior reading. The Vulgate and some Syriac versions read Beelzebub. For a more comprehensive presentation of the textual evidence, see W. E. M. Aitken ("Beelzebul," *JBL* 31 [1912] 34-35).

2. Aitken, "Beelzebul," 36; Lloyd Gaston, "Beelzebul," *TZ* 18 (1962) 247; Vincent Taylor, *The Gospel According to Mark* (London: MacMillan, 1966) 239; E. C. B. MacLaurin, "Beelzeboul," *NovT* 20 (1978) 156.

3. H. L. Strack and P. Billerbeck, *Kommentar zum neuen Testament aus Talmud und Midrasch* (Munich: C. H. Beck'sche, 1956) vol. 1, 632. Burton Easton (*The Gospel According to St. Luke* [New York: Charles Scribner's Sons, 1928] 180) also understood -*zeboul* to mean "dung," but it is unclear to me what he thought -*zeboul* cacophemistically replaces. M. -J. Lagrange (*Evangile selon Saint Marc* [Paris: J. Gabalda, 1911] 64) thought that the original name of the god was *Baʿal Zĕbûb*, "Baal

links Beelzebul with the Aramaic expression *bĕᶜēl dĕbābāʾ*, "adversary, enemy."[4] It is the purpose of this appendix to demonstrate the shortcomings of the first two propositions, and to provide new argumentation in support of the third, and hitherto least accepted, proposal.

In order to support the first theory, W. E. M. Aitken[5] and Lloyd Gaston[6] rallied convincing circumstantial evidence indicating that the author of Matt 10:25 understood *-zĕbûl* to mean "dwelling." More specifically they demonstrated, by examination of the LXX, Qumranic and rabbinic sources, that *zĕbûl* in those contexts was used in reference to the heavenly dwelling of God, or its earthly representation, the temple. They consequently translated *Beelzeboul* as "lord of the heavenly dwelling," a translation which creates a greater problem than the one it purports to solve. If Beelzebul meant "lord of the heavenly dwelling," how did such a name become attached to the figure Satan?

The proponents of the "master of the house" theory are no doubt correct in saying that Matt 10:25 offers an explanation of the name Beelzebul. However, it does not follow that the explanation offered in Matt 10:25 is the historically correct etymology of the name, or that it provides an indispensable clue to the

----

of the flies" [sic]. For the reason why *zîbbûl* cannot be a pun on *zĕbûl*, "house," see below.

4. E. K. A. Riehm, *Handwörterbuch des biblischen Altertums* (Leipzig: Velhagen, 1893) Band 1, 195-196; Alan H. McNeile, *The Gospel According to Matthew* (London: MacMillan, 1915) 143; Adolf Schlatter, *Der Evangelist Matthaüs* (Stuttgart: Calwer, 1957) 343. Note the title *ho echthros*, "the enemy," in Matt 13:39.

5. "Beelzebul," 36-40.

6. "Beelzebul," 247-250.

mechanism by which Beelzebul became identified with Satan. To illustrate my first objection, let us consider the name Melchizedek, which is explained by the author of Heb 7:2 to mean "king of righteousness." As Fitzmyer[7] and Delcor[8] have shown, the original meaning of Melchizedek was, most probably, "[the god] Ṣdk is my king." Likewise, the author of Matt 10:25 provides an explanation suited more to his own exegetical agenda than to historical accuracy. As we know from Ugarit, *zbl* was an epithet of Baal which, as Moshe Held[9] argued, meant "prince." If we assume, as many biblical scholars do in light of the Ugaritic evidence, that MT's *baʿal zĕbûb* (2 Kgs 1:2,3,6,16) replaces an original **baʿal zĕbûl*,[10] then *Bʿl Zbl* was traditionally known as the name of a foreign, and therefore abhorred, deity. Given that all foreign deities had the potential of being construed as demons (LXX Ps 95:5; 1 Cor 10:20),[11] *Bʿl Zbl* had the

----

7. "'Now This Melchizedek...' (Heb 7,1)," *CBQ* 25 (1963) 311-312.

8. "Melchizedek from Genesis to the Qumran Texts and the Epistle to the Hebrews," *JSJ* 2 (1971) 115-116.

9. "The Root ZBL/SBL in Akkadian, Ugaritic, and Biblical Hebrew," *JAOS* 88 (1968) 92.

10. W. Foerster (*TDNT* vol. 1, 606) even suggested that the synoptic sources had available to them a textual tradition which preserved the reading *bʿl zbl*. Although speculative, Foerster's suggestion is attractive, given the plurality of textual traditions in circulation at the time. Cf. F. M. Cross, "The Contribution of Qumran Discoveries to the Study of the Biblical Text," in F. M. Cross and S. Talmon (eds.), *Qumran and the History of the Biblical Text* (Cambridge: Harvard, 1975) 278-292 (= *IEJ* 16 (1966) 81-95). However, it is also possible that the identification of the two names was confined to oral tradition.

11. Cf. Gaston, "Beelzebul," 253; Joseph Fitzmyer, *The Gospel According to Luke*, x-xxiv (AB 28a; Garden City:

potential of becoming demonized simply by virtue of his status in the HB as a foreign deity. Thus we need not affirm Matt 10:25's explication of the name Beelzebul as the mechanism by which this deity became identified with Satan.

The unsuitability of the first proposal's "lord of the heavenly dwelling" as a synonym for Satan provided an impetus[12] for the second proposal, which sees in Greek -*zeboul* a reflection of Aramaic *zîbbûl*, "dung." Lagrange[13] identified -*zeboul*, with the meaning "dung," as a cacophemistic substitution for *zĕbûb*, "fly," which he accepted as an original component of the name of the god referred to in 2 Kings 1. But if we understand *zĕbûb*, "fly," to be itself a derisive substitution for *zĕbûl*, "prince," then "dung" becomes a cacopheme replacing something that is already contumely. Furthermore, as Gaston[14] pointed out, *zîbbûl* is not an "independent" word, but rather a cacophemistic substitution specifically for *zîbbûaḥ*, "sacrifice." That is, *zîbbûl* combines the consonants of the word *zebel*, "dung," with the vocalization pattern of *zîbbûaḥ*, "sacrifice," to create a word used *only* as a cacophemism for "sacrifice." Thus the Greek -*zeboul*, if intended to convey the meaning "dung," could only do so if a hypothetical "Beelzibbuaḥ" was presupposed.[15]

Doubleday, 1985) 920.

12. For example, Strack and Billerbeck, *Kommentar*, 632.

13. *Evangile*, 64.

14. "Beelzebul," 251-252.

15. Fitzmyer (*Luke*, 920) raises the additional objection that *zîbbûl*, "dung," cannot be documented in contemporary Aramaic.

Strack and Billerbeck, no doubt aware of the restricted usage of *zîbbûl*, insisted that Greek -*zeboul* had nothing whatsoever to do with the root *zbb*, and rather should be understood exclusively in connection with the root *zbḥ*, "sacrifice."[16] The primary objection to this proposal is the Greek spelling -*zeboul*, which does not easily suggest a transliteration of *zîbbûl*.[17] Furthermore this solution, like the solution proposed by the first theory, replaces a problem with yet another problem; we arrive at the designation "Beelzibbuaḥ," which is unattested as a divine epithet. Strack and Billerbeck are simply trading one obscurity for another.[18]

Whereas the etymology "lord of the heavenly dwelling" is inappropriate for a name applied to Satan, and "lord of dung" is unacceptable because of the Greek spelling and because it leads us to an obscure "Beelzibbuaḥ," the proposal to connect Beelzebul with *bĕʿēl dĕbābāʾ*, "enemy," has the advantage of supplying a semantically plausible reason for the equation of Beelzebul and Satan. The reason that this last proposal has received such little support is that the arguments used in its favor by its defenders simply have not been sound. I shall review these arguments and the objections they have engendered, and then propose another line of argumentation.

Lagrange[19] began by positing that "Beelzebub"

----

16. Strack and Billerbeck, *Kommentar*, 632.

17. Gaston "Beelzebul," 251.

18. Cf. Gaston, "Beelzebul," 251.

19. *Evangile*, 64.

reflects the primitive reading. He argued that the Aramaic equivalent of Hebrew z̲b̲b̲, that is, d̲b̲b̲ʾ,[20] could have been construed either as "fly" or as "enemy." Strack and Billerbeck[21] objected to this line of reasoning because Beelzeboul is the textually preferable reading, and I would not disagree on this point. McNeile[22] and Schlatter[23] argued that the textually preferable -z̲eb̲ou̲l̲ is an intentional corruption of d̲ĕb̲ā̲b̲ā̲ʾ, but as Aitken[24] pointed out, no suggestion has been offered as to why bĕʿēl d̲ĕb̲ā̲b̲ā̲ʾ, "the enemy," which is a perfectly understandable designation for Satan, would have been intentionally corrupted. Even if one allows the implausible suggestion that b̲>l̲ took place simply in order to fascilitate Greek pronunciation,[25] one is still left without an explanation for the supposed movement from d̲ to z̲. Thus this line of reasoning too must be dismissed as inadequate.

　　　　Given the textual evidence, we must accept Beelzeboul as the starting point. Aitken[26] and Gaston[27] objected to any connection between Beelzebul

----

20. Hebrew z̲ and Aramaic d̲ can be the respective realizations of proto-Semitic *d̲̣. Arabic d̲̣ubab̲, "fly," confirms the correspondence in this case.

21. Kommentar, 631.

22. The Gospel, 143.

23. Der Evangelist, 343.

24. "Beelzebul," 51.

25. Cf. the examples given by Strack and Billerbeck (Kommentar, 632).

26. "Beelzebul," 52.

27. "Beelzebul," 251 n.16.

and _bĕʿēl dĕbābāʾ_ because they found no reason to suppose that the NT authors knew that _zĕbûb_ was a perversion of _zĕbûl_. On the contrary, I would argue that _zĕbûb_ and _zĕbûl_ were inextricably linked in the tradition by the substitution of _zĕbûb_ for _zĕbûl_ in 2 Kings 1. As _zîbbûl_ was a cacophemistic replacement expressly for _zîbbûaḥ_, so _baʿal zĕbûb_, the "fly god," could be used as a derisive reference _only_ to _Bʿl Zbl_. This presupposition is made even more attractive by the fact that the Vulgate and Syriac witnesses, both with close affinities to Jewish tradition, chose to replace _Beelzeboul_ with Beelzebub.

Beelzebul, then, is inextricably bound to Beelzebub. The Aramaic equivalent of Hebrew _zĕbûb_, "fly," is _dîbābāʾ_. This in turn suggested a word play, a folk-etymological pun on the expression _bĕʿēl dĕbābāʾ_, "enemy."[28] As a foreign deity, and particularly as a foreign deity familiar from traditional literature, _Bʿl Zbl_ was a candidate for becoming regarded as a demon, and because the Aramaic version of his name allowed such a tantalizing word play, he became identified with Satan, the archetypal enemy. Although the mediating capacity of _bĕʿēl dĕbābāʾ_ is not explicit in the NT sources, it should be noted that in Syriac, _bĕʿēl dĕbābāʾ_ signifies not only "adversary" in general, but also, specifically, the devil.

----

28. Strack and Billerbeck (_Kommentar_, 631) rejected the possibility of a word play because they found it questionable whether Aramaic _dîbābāʾ_, "fly," was a bonafide equivalent of Hebrew _zĕbûb_. As evidence, they pointed out that the Targum to 2 Kings 1 does not replace Hebrew _zĕbûb_ with Aramaic _dîbābāʾ_, but rather lets the Hebrew word stand. They neglected to point out, however, that _Tg. Yer._ Lev 11:20, _Tg. Isa_ 7:18, and _Tg. Ket._ Qoh 10:1 all use Aramaic _dîbābāʾ_ in place of Hebrew _zĕbûb_.

One final point of possible semantic contact between *bĕʿēl dĕbābāʾ* and Satan should be noted. *Bĕʿēl dĕbābāʾ* is a loan into Aramaic from the Akkadian expression *bēl dabābi*,[29] which meant both "enemy" and "accuser in court." The Aramaic documents from Elephantine clearly preserve the juridical thrust of Akkadian *dabābu*, for instance in the hendiadys *dyn wdbb*, "formal process, legal suit."[30] Although the term *bʿl dbb* is not found at Elephantine, the fact that *dbb* appears in legal usage might indicate that *bʿl dbb* also was borrowed within a forensic context, and was retained with an as yet unevidenced legal connotation.[31]

If *bĕʿēl dĕbābāʾ* could also signify a legal accuser, this would provide an even more compelling reason to link Beelzebul and Satan. If we suppose that *bĕʿēl dĕbābāʾ* and Satan shared not only a general

----

29. Stephen A. Kaufman, *The Akkadian Influences on Aramaic* (Chicago: University of Chicago, 1974) 42-43.

30. Yochanan Muffs, *Studies in the Aramaic Legal Papyri from Elephantine* (Leiden: Brill, 1969) 30-33, 234.

31. Kaufman (*Influences*, 42) , in rejecting the possibility that *bĕʿēl dĕbābāʾ* ever had any legal connotation, styles the Elephantine community as employing legal terminology that was distinct from the main stream. But as Muffs (*Studies*, 189, 191) pointed out, the settlers at Elephantine brought their legal vocabulary with them, and hence we can infer that *dbb* had a legal connotation in the Imperial Aramaic of the period as well as at Elephantine.

Kaufman also asserts that *bʿl dynʾ* was the "usual expression" for "adversary in court," yet to my knowledge, the only evidence which predates the standard targumic and mishnaic sources is a single reference, 4QEnGiants^{c} 6:5 (*bʿl dyn*). Although this reference proves that *bʿl dyn did* exist as a term for "accuser," it does not prove that *bĕʿēl dĕbābāʾ* did not exist, either side by side with *bʿl dyn*, or within a community other than the one at Qumran.

inimical disposition, but also, more specifically, functioned as accusers, then the semantic tie would be sufficiently tight to turn a potentially tantalizing word play into an irresistible one.

SELECTED BIBLIOGRAPHY

Abusch, Israel Tzvi. "Studies in the History and Interpretation of Some Akkadian Incantations and Prayers Against Witchcraft." Ph.D. dissertation, Harvard, 1972.

Abrahams, Roger D. "Proverbs and Proverbial Expressions," R. Dorson (ed.), Folklore and Folklife, 117-128. Chicago: University of Chicago, 1972.

Ackerman, James. "An Exegetical Study of Psalm 82." Th.D. dissertation, Harvard, 1966.

Ackroyd, Peter R. Exile and Restoration. OTL; Philadelphia: Westminster, 1968.

__________. First and Second Chronicles, Ezra, Nehemia. London: SCM, 1973.

__________. "The Old Testament in the Making," P. R. Ackroyd (ed.), The Cambridge History of the Bible, vol. 1, 67-112. Cambridge: Cambridge University, 1971.

Aitken, W. E. M. "Beelzebul," JBL 31 (1912) 34-53.

Albertz, Rainer. Persönliche Frömmigkeit und offizielle Religion. Stuttgart: Calwer, 1978.

Albright, W. F. "The Home of Balaam," JAOS 35 (1917) 386-390.

__________. "The Oracles of Balaam," JBL 63 (1944) 207-233.

__________. "Some Important Recent Discoveries: Alphabetic Origins and the Idrimi Statue," BASOR 118 (April, 1950) 11-20.

Barr, James. "Etymology and the Old Testament," OTS 19 (1974) 4-17.

__________. The Semantics of Biblical Language. London: Oxford University, 1961.

Barré, M. L. "A Note on Job 19:25," VT 29 (1979) 107-110.

Bauer, Hans, and Leander, Pontus. Historische Grammatik der hebräischen Sprache. Halle: Niemayer, 1918-1922;

reprinted, Hildesheim: Georg Olms, 1962.

Begrich, Joachim. "Sōfēr und Mazkîr," ZAW 58 (1940/41) 1-29.

Beuken, W. A. M. Haggai-Sacharja 1-8. Assen: Van Gorcum, 1967.

Beyse, Karl Martin. Serubbabel und die Königserwartungen der Propheten Haggai und Sacharja. Stuttgart: Calwer, 1972.

Birkeland, Harris. Die Feinde des Individuums in der israelitischen Psalmenliteratur. Oslo: Grøndahl and Sons, 1933.

Boecker, Hans J. "Erwägungen zum Amt des Mazkir," TZ 17 (1961) 212-216.

__________. Law and the Administration of Justice in the Old Testament and Ancient East. Minneapolis: Ausburg, 1980.

__________. Redeformen des Rechtsleben im Alten Testament. Neukirchen-Vluyn: Neukirchener, 1964.

Bohannan, Paul. "The Differing Realms of Law," P. Bohannan (ed.), Law and Warfare, 43-56. New York: Natural History, 1967.

Boling, Robert G. and Wright, G. Ernest. Joshua. AB 6; Garden City: Doubleday, 1982.

Bič, Miloš. Das Buch Sacharja. Berlin: Evangelische Verlagsanstalt, 1962.

Braun, R. "Chronicles, Ezra and Nehemiah: Theology and Literary History," J. A. Emerton (ed.), Studies in the Historical Books of the Old Testament, 52-64. VTSup 30; Leiden: Brill, 1979.

Bright, John. "The Organization and Administration of the Israelite Empire," F. M. Cross et al. (eds.), Magnalia Dei, 193-208. New York: Doubleday, 1976.

Brockelmann, C. Grundriss der vergleichenden Grammatik der semitischen Sprachen. Berlin: Reuther und Reichard, 1908.

Brock-Unte, Albert. "Der Feind: Das alttestamentliche Satangestalt im Licht der sozialen Verhältnisse des nahen Orients," Klio 28 (1935) 219-237.

Brown, Raymond E. *The Gospel according to John*, (i-xii). AB 29; Garden City: Doubleday, 1966.

Buccellati, Georgio. *The Amorites of the Ur III Period*. Naples: Istituto Orientale, 1966.

Buttenweiser, Moses. *The Book of Job*. New York: MacMillan, 1922.

Canney, Maurice A. "The Hebrew *mēlîṣ*," *AJSL* 40 (1923/24) 135-137.

Carpenter, J. Estlin, and Harford-Battersby, G. *The Hexateuch*. New York: Longmans, Green and Co., 1900.

Caspari, D. W. *Die Samuelbücher*. KAT 7; Leipzig: Scholl, 1926.

Coogan, Michael D. "Canaanite Origins and Lineage: Reflections on the Religion of Ancient Israel," P. D. Miller, P. D. Hanson, and S. D. McBride (eds.), *Ancient Israelite Religion: Essays in Honor of Frank Moore Cross*. Philadelphia: Fortress, 1987.

Cross, Frank Moore. *The Ancient Library of Qumran and Modern Biblical Studies*. Garden City: Doubleday, 1961.

__________. *Canaanite Myth and Hebrew Epic*. Cambridge: Harvard University, 1973.

__________. "The Council of Yahweh in Second Isaiah," *JNES* 12 (1953) 274-277.

__________. "The Epic Traditions of Early Israel: Epic Narrative and the Reconstruction of Early Israelite Institutions," R. E. Friedman (ed.), *The Poet and the Historian*, 13-39. HSM 26; Chico: Scholars, 1983.

__________. "A Reconstruction of the Judean Restoration," *JBL* 94 (1975) 3-18.

Curtis, E. L., and Madsen, A. A. *The Book of Chronicles*. ICC; Edinburgh: T. and T. Clark, 1910.

Curtis, John Briggs. "On Job's Witness in Heaven," *JBL* 102 (1983) 549-562.

Dahood, Mitchell. *Psalms III: 101-150*. AB 17a; Garden City: Doubleday, 1970.

Davidson, A. B., and Toy, C. H. "The Book of Job," Ralph E. Hone (ed.), *The Voice out of the Whirlwind: The Book of Job*. San Fransisco: Chandler, 1960.

Day, Peggy L. "Abishai the *śāṭān* in 2 Sam 19:17-24," *CBQ* 49 (1987) 543-547.

Dégh, Linda. "Folk Narrative," R. Dorson (ed.), *Folklore and Folklife*, 53-84. Chicago: University of Chicago, 1972.

Delcor, M. "Balaᶜam Pâtôrâh, 'interprète de songes' au pays d'Ammon, d'après Num 22:5: les témoignages épigraphiques parallèles," *Semitica* 32 (1982) 89-91.

__________. "Le texte de Deir ᶜAllā et les oracles bibliques de Balaᶜam," VTSup 32 (1980) 52-73.

__________. "Melchizedek from Genesis to the Qumran Texts and the Epistle to the Hebrews," *JSJ* 2 (1971) 115-135.

Dhorme, Paul. *Le livre de Job*. Paris: Gabalda, 1926.

Dion, Paul. "The Angel with the Drawn Sword (2 [sic] Chr 21,16): An Exercise in Restoring the Balance of Text Criticism *and* Attention to Context," *ZAW* 97 (1985) 114-117.

Driver, S. R., and Gray, G. B. *The Book of Job*. ICC 14; New York: Charles Scribner's Sons, 1921.

Drower, E. S., and Macuch, R. *A Mandaic Dictionary*. Oxford: Clarendon, 1963.

Duhm, Hans. *Die bösen Geister im Alten Testament*. Tübingen: J.C.B. Mohr, 1904.

Easton, Burton. *The Gospel According to Saint Luke*. New York: Scribner's, 1928.

Eichrodt, W. "Vom Symbol zum Typos," *TZ* 13 (1957) 509-522.

Elliger, Kurt. *Die zwölfe kleinen Propheten*. Göttingen: Vandenhoeck und Ruprecht, 1975.

Falk, Zeev W. "Hebrew Legal Terms," *JSS* 5 (1960) 350-354.

__________. "Hebrew Legal Terms: II," *JSS* 12 (1967) 241-244.

__________. "Hebrew Legal Terms: III," *JSS* 14 (1969) 39-44.

Fishbane, Michael. "Jeremiah 4:23-26 and Job 3:3-13: A

Recovered Use of the Creation Pattern," _VT_ 21 (1971) 151-167.

Fitzmyer, Joseph. "Now This Melchizedek...(Heb 7,1)," _CBQ_ 25 (1963) 305-321.

__________. _The Gospel According to Luke_, x-xxiv. AB 28a; Garden City: Doubleday, 1985.

Flanagan, James W. "Court History or Succession Document? A Study of 2 Samuel 9-20 and 1 Kings 1-2," _JBL_ 91 (1972) 172-181.

Frankena, R. "The Vassal Treaties of Esarhaddon and the Dating of Deuteronomy," _OTS_ 14 (1965) 122-154.

Freedman, David Noel. "The Chronicler's Purpose," _CBQ_ 23 (1961) 436-442.

Frye, Richard N. _The Heritage of Persia_. New York: World, 1963.

Fullerton, Kemper. "Double Entendre in the First Speech of Eliphaz," _JBL_ 49 (1930) 320-374.

Fuss, Werner. "2 Samuel 24," _ZAW_ 74 (1962) 145-161.

Galling, Kurt. _Die Bücher der Chronik, Ezra, Nehemia_. Göttingen: Vandenhoeck und Ruprecht, 1954.

__________. "Das Gemeindegesetz in Deuteronomium 23," _Festschrift für A. Bertholet_, W. Baumgartner et al. (eds.), 176-191. Tübingen: J.C.B. Mohr, 1950.

__________. _Studien zur Geschichte Israels im persischen Zeitalter_. Tübingen: J.C.B. Mohr, 1964.

Gaster, T. H. "Satan," _IDB_ vol. 4, 224-228.

Gaston, Lloyd. "Beelzebul," _TZ_ 18 (1962) 247-255.

Gelston, A. "The Foundation of the Second Temple," _VT_ 16 (1966) 232-235.

Gemser, B. "The _Rîb_--or Controversy--Pattern in Hebrew Mentality," VTSup 3 (1955) 120-137.

Gerber, W. J. _Die hebräischen Verba denominativa_. Leipzig: J. C. Hinrichs, 1896.

Good, Edwin M. _Irony in the Old Testament_. Philadelphia: Westminster, 1965.

__________. "Job and the Literary Task: A Response," Soundings 56 (1973) 470-484.

Gordis, Robert. The Book of Job: Commentary, New Translation, and Special Studies. New York: Jewish Theological Seminary, 1978.

Greengus, Samuel. Old Babylonian Tablets from Ishchali and Vicinity. Istanbul: Dutch Historical-Archaeological Inst., 1979.

Grill, Severin. "Synonyme Engelnamen im Alten Testament," TZ 18 (1962) 241-246.

Gross, Walter. Bileam: Literar- und formkritische Untersuchung der Prosa in Num 22-24. München: Kösel, 1974.

Gunkel, Hermann. Das Märchen im Alten Testament. Tübingen: J.C.B. Mohr, 1921.

__________. Die Psalmen. HKAT; Göttingen: Vandenhoeck und Ruprecht, 1926.

Haag, Herbert. Teufelsglaube. Tübingen: Katzmann, 1974.

Habel, Norman C. The Book of Job: A Commentary. OTL; Philadelphia: Westminster, 1985.

__________. "The Narrative Art of Job," JSOT 27 (1983) 101-111.

__________. "'Only the Jackal is my Friend': on Friends and Redeemers in Job," Int 31 (1977) 227-236.

Hackett, Jo Ann. The Balaam Text from Deir ʿAllā. HSM 31; Chico: Scholars, 1984.

Hallo, William. "Individual Prayer in Sumerian: The Continuity of a Tradition," JAOS 88 (1968) 71-89.

Halpern, Baruch, and Huehnergard, John. "El-Amarna Letter 252," Or 51 (1982) 227-230.

Hanson, Paul. The Dawn of Apocalyptic. Philadelphia: Fortress, 1979.

__________. "In Defiance of Death: Zechariah's Symbolic Universe," Marvin Pope Festschrift. New Haven: Four Quarters, forthcoming.

__________. "Zechariah, Book of," G. Butterick (ed.), Interpreter's Dictionary of the Bible, supp. vol.,

982-983. Nashville: Abingdon, 1976.

Harrelson, Walter. "The Trial of the High Priest Joshua: Zechariah 3," Eretz-Israel 16 (1982) 116*-124*.

Harvey, J. "Le 'Rîb Pattern,' réquisitoire prophétique sur la rupture de l'alliance," Biblica 43 (1962) 172-196.

Hatch, Edwin and Redpath, Henry. A Concordance to the Septuagint. Graz: Akademische Druck-U. Verlagsanstalt, 1954.

Haupt, Paul. "The Visions of Zechariah," JBL 32 (1913) 107-122.

Heater, Homer. A Septuagint Translation Technique in the Book of Job. CBQ Monographs 11; Washington: Catholic Biblical Assn., 1982.

Held, Moshe. "The Root ZBL/SBL in Akkadian, Ugaritic, and Biblical Hebrew," JAOS 88 (1968) 90-96.

Hertzberg, H. W. 1 and 2 Samuel: A Commentary. London: SCM, 1964.

Hirschfeld, H. "Bemerkungen zum Verbum denominativum im Hebräischen," Monatsschrift 69 (1925) 223-230.

Hoffman, Yair. "The Relation Between the Prologue and the Speech Cycles in Job," VT 31 (1981) 160-170.

Holbert, J. C. "'The Skies Will Uncover his Iniquity:' Satire in the Second Speech of Zophar (Job 20)," VT 31 (1981) 171-179.

Horst, F. "Die Visionsschilderungen der alttestamentlichen Propheten," EvT 20 (1960) 193-205.

Huehnergard, John. See Halpern, Baruch.

Huffmon, H. B. "The Covenant Lawsuit in the Prophets," JBL 78 (1959) 285-295.

Hurvitz, Avi. "The Date of the Prose-Tale of Job Linguistically Reconsidered," HTR 67 (1974) 17-34.

Irwin, W. A. "The Elihu Speeches in the Criticism of the Book of Job," JR 17 (1937) 37-47.

__________. "Job's Redeemer," JBL 81 (1962) 217-229.

Jackson, Bernard S. Essays in Jewish and Comparative Legal History. Leiden: Brill, 1975.

Jacobsen, Thorkild. "Primitive Democracy in Ancient Mesopotamia," *JNES* 2 (1943) 159-172.

__________. *The Treasures of Darkness*. New Haven: Yale, 1976.

Jacobson, Richard. "Satanic Semiotics, Jobian Jurisprudence," *Semeia* 19 (1981) 63-71.

Janzen, J. Gerald. *Job*. Atlanta: John Knox, 1985.

Japhet, Sara. "The Supposed Common Authorship of Chronicles and Ezra-Nehemia Investigated Anew," *VT* 18 (1968) 330-371.

Jenks, Alan W. *The Elohist and North Israelite Tradition*. Missoula: Scholars, 1977.

Jepsen, Alfred. "Kleine Beitrage zum Zwölfeprophetenbuch III: 4. Sacharja," *ZAW* 20 (1945-1948) 95-114.

Jeremias, Christian. *Die Nachtgesichte des Sacharja*. Göttingen: Vandenhoeck und Ruprecht, 1977.

Johansson, Nils. *Parakletoi*. Lund: Gleerup, 1940.

Joüon, Paul. *Grammaire de l'hébreu biblique*. Rome: Pontifical Biblical Institute, 1923.

Kaufman, Stephen A. *The Akkadian Influences on Aramaic*. Chicago: University of Chicago, 1974.

__________. "Review Article: The Aramaic Texts from Deir ᶜAllā," *BASOR* 239 (1980) 71-74.

Kaupel, Heinrich. *Die Dämonen im Alten Testament*. Augsberg: Dr. Benno Filser, 1930.

Kissane, Edward. *The Book of Job*. New York: Sheed and Ward, 1946.

Kittel, Rudolph. *Die Bücher der Chronik*. HAT 6; Göttingen: Vandenhoeck und Ruprecht, 1902.

Kluger, Rivkah Schärf. "Die Gestalt des Satans im Alten Testament," C. G. Jung (ed.), *Symbolik des Geistes*. Zurich: Rascher, 1948. Republished as *Satan in the Old Testament*. Evanston: Northwestern University, 1967.

Knight, Douglas A. "Cosmogony and Order in the Hebrew Tradition," Robin W. Lovin (ed.), *Cosmogony and Ethical Order*, 133-157. Chicago: University of Chicago, 1985.

Kohler, Ludwig. Hebrew Man. New York: Abingdon, 1956.

Kraus, Hans-Joachim. Psalmen, 2 vols.. BKAT; Neukirchen: Neukirchener, 1960.

Kupper, J. R. "Le recensement dans le textes de Mari," A. Parrot (ed.), Studia Mariana. Leiden: Brill, 1950.

Lagrange, M.-J. Evangile selon Saint Marc. Paris: Gabalda, 1911.

Lambert, W. G. and Gurney, O. R. "The Sultantepe Tablets: The Poem of the Righteous Sufferer," Anatolian Studies 4 (1954) 65-99.

Landsberger, Benno. "Remarks on the Archive of the Soldier Ubarum," JCS 9 (1955) 121-131.

Lane, Edward William. An Arabic English Lexicon. London: Williams and Norgate, 1872.

Lemke, Werner E. "The Synoptic Problem in the Chronicler's History," HTR 58 (1965) 349-363.

__________. "Synoptic Studies in the Chronicler's History." Ph.D. dissertation, Harvard University, 1963.

Levine, Baruch A. "Review Article: The Deir ʿAllā Plaster Inscriptions," JAOS 101 (1981) 195-205.

Limberg, James. "The Root ryb and the Prophetic Lawsuit Speeches," JBL 88 (1969) 291-304.

Lods, Adolphe. "Les origines de la figure de satan, ses fonctions à la cour céleste," Mélanges syriens offerts à Monsieur René Dussaud, vol. 2, 649-660. Paris: Paul Geuthner, 1939.

Long, Burke O. "Etymological Etiology and the DT Historian," CBQ 31 (1969) 35-41.

__________. "Reports of Visions Among the Prophets," JBL 95 (1976) 353-365.

Loretz, Oswald. Die Psalmen, 2 vols.. Neukirchen-Vluyn: Neukirchener, 1979.

Lüthi, Max. Once Upon A Time: On the Nature of Fairy Tales. Bloomington: Indiana University, 1970.

Macholz, Georg C. "Die Stellung des Königs in der israelitischen Gerichtsverfassung," ZAW 84 (1972)

157-182.

MacKenzie, R. A. F. "The Purpose of the Yahweh Speeches in the Book of Job," Bib 40 (1959) 435-445.

MacLaurin, E. C. B. "Beelzeboul," NovT 20 (1978) 156-160.

Malamat, A. "Aspects of the Foreign Policies of David and Solomon," JNES 22 (1963) 1-17.

Mangan, Celine. 1-2 Chronicles, Ezra, Nehemia. Wilmington: Michael Glazier, 1982.

Marti, Karl. "Zwei Studien zu Sacharja: I. Der Ursprung des Satans," TSK 65 (1892) 207-245.

Mauchline, J. 1 and 2 Samuel. London: Oliphants, 1971.

May, Herbert G. "A Key to the Interpretation of Zechariah's Visions," JBL 57 (1938) 173-184.

Mayes, A. D. H. Deuteronomy. CB; London: Oliphants, 1979.

McCarter, P. Kyle. "The Apology of David," JBL 99 (1980) 489-504.

__________. "The Balaam Texts from Deir ʿAllā: The First Combination," BASOR 239 (1980) 49-60.

__________. "Rib-Adda's Appeal to Aziru (EA 162, 1-21)," OrAnt 12 (1973) 15-18.

__________. 1 Samuel. AB 8; Garden City: Doubleday, 1980.

__________. 2 Samuel. AB 9; Garden City: Doubleday, 1984.

McCarthy, Dennis J. "The Wrath of Yahweh and the Structural Unity of the Deuteronomistic History," J. L. Crenshaw and J. T. Willis (eds.), Essays in Old Testament Ethics, 97-110. New York: Ktav, 1974.

McKenzie, Steven Linn. "The Chronicler's Use of the Deuteronomistic History." Th.D. dissertation, Harvard University, 1983.

__________. The Chronicler's Use of the Deuteronomistic History. HSM 33; Atlanta: Scholars, 1985.

McNeile, Alan H. The Gospel According to Matthew. London: MacMillan, 1915.

Meek, T. J. "Job 19:25-27," VT 6 (1956) 100-103.

Mettinger, Tryggve N. D. Solomonic State Officials. Lund: Gleerup, 1971.

Meyers, Carol L. and Eric M. Haggai, Zechariah 1-8. AB 25B; Garden City: Doubleday, 1987.

Mitchell, H. G. Haggai, Zechariah, Malachi and Jonah. ICC; Edinburgh: T. and T. Clark, 1912.

Moran, William L. "Notes on the Hymn to Marduk in Ludlul bēl Nēmeqi," JAOS 103 (1981) 255-260.

Moore, Rick D. "The Integrity of the Book of Job," CBQ 45 (1983) 17-31.

Moscati, Sabatino. An Introduction to the Comparative Grammar of the Semitic Languages. Wiesbaden: Harrassowitz, 1964.

Mosis, Rudolph. Untersuchungen zur Theologie des chronistischen Geschichtswerkes. Freiburg: Herder, 1973.

Mowinckel, Sigmund. "Hiob's gōʾēl und Zeuge im Himmel," Karl Budde (ed.), Vom Alten Testament, 207-212. BZAW 41; Giessen: Alfred Töpelmann, 1925.

__________. "Der Ursprung der Bilʿāmsage," ZAW 48 (1930) 233-271.

__________. "Die Vorstellungen des Spätjudentums von heiligen Geist als Fürsprecher und der johanneische Paraklet," ZNW 32 (1933) 97-130.

Muffs, Yochanan. Studies in the Aramaic Legal Papyri from Elephantine. Leiden: Brill, 1969.

Mullen, E. Theodore. The Assembly of the Gods: The Divine Council in Canaanite and Early Hebrew Literature. HSM 24; Chico: Scholars, 1980.

Muller, H.-P. "Die aramäische Inshrift von Deir ʿAllā und die alteren Bileamssprüche," ZAW 94 (1982) 214-244.

Myers, Jacob. 1 Chronicles. AB 12; Garden City: Doubleday, 1965.

Nasr, Seyyed T. Essai sur l'histoire du droit Persan dès l'origine à l'invasion arabe. Paris: Mechelinck, 1933.

Newsome, James D. "Toward a New Understanding of the

Chronicler and his Purposes," JBL 94 (1975) 201-217.

Nickelsburg, George W. E. Jewish Literature Between the Bible and the Mishnah. Philadelphia: Fortress, 1981.

Niditch, Susan. The Symbolic Vision in Biblical Tradition. HSM 30; Chico: Scholars, 1980.

North, Robert. "Theology of the Chronicler," JBL 82 (1963) 369-381.

Noth, Martin. The Deuteronomistic History. JSOT 15; Sheffield: JSOT, 1981.

__________. A History of Pentateuchal Traditions. Chico: Scholars, 1981.

__________. Numbers. OTL; London: SCM, 1968.

Nougayrol, Jean. Ugaritica V (= Mission de Ras Shamra, tome 16). Paris: Imprimerie Nationale, 1968.

Nowack, W. Die kleinen Propheten. HKAT 3; Göttingen: Vandenhoeck und Ruprecht, 1922.

Olmstead, A. T. History of the Persian Empire. Chicago: University of Chicago, 1948.

Oppenheim, Leo. "The Eyes of the Lord," JAOS 88 (1968) 173-180.

Peckham, Brian. The Composition of the Deuteronomistic History. HSM 35; Atlanta: Scholars, 1985.

Petersen, David L. Haggai and Zechariah 1-8: A Commentary. OTL; Philadelphia: Fortress, 1984.

__________. Late Israelite Prophecy: Studies in the Deuteroprophetic Literature and in Chronicles. Missoula: Scholars, 1977.

Petitjean, Albert. "La mission de Zorobabel et la reconstruction du temple: Zach., III, 8-10," ETL 42 (1966) 40-71.

__________. Les oracles du proto-Zecharie. Paris: Gabalda, 1969.

Polzin, Robert. "The Framework of the Book of Job," Int 28 (1974) 182-200.

Pope, Marvin. Job: A Commentary. AB 15; Garden City: Doubleday, 1965.

Power, William J. A. "A Study of Irony in the Book of Job." Ph.D. dissertation, U. of Toronto, 1961.

Rad, Gerhard von. Deuteronomy. OTL; Philadelphia: Westminster, 1966.

__________. "diabolos," TDNT, vol. 2, 72-81.

__________. Das Geschichtsbild des chronistischen Werkes. Stuttgart: W. Kohlhammer, 1930.

Ramsey, George W. "Speech Forms in Hebrew Law and the Prophetic Oracles," JBL 96 (1977) 45-58.

Redford, D. B. "Studies in Relations Between Palestine and Egypt During the First Millennium B.C.: The Taxation System of Solomon," J. W. Wevers and D. B. Redford (eds.), Studies in the Ancient Palestinian World, 141-156. Toronto: University of Toronto, 1972.

Reventlow, H. Graf. "Das Amt des Mazkir. Zur Rechtsstruktur des öffentlichen Lebens in Israel," TZ 15 (1959) 161-175.

Richardson, H. Neil. "Some Notes on lîṣ and its Derivatives," VT 5 (1955) 163-179.

__________. "Two Addenda to 'Some Notes on lîṣ and its Derivatives,'" VT 6 (1956) 434-436.

Ricoeur, Paul. The Symbolism of Evil. Boston: Beacon, 1967.

Rignell, Lars. Die Nachtgesichte des Sacharja. Lund: Ohlssons, 1950.

Roberts, Simon A. Order and Dispute: An Introduction to Legal Anthropology. New York: St. Martin's, 1979.

Robertson, David. "The Book of Job: A Literary Study," Soundings 56 (1973) 446-469.

Robinson, H. Wheeler. "The Council of Yahweh," JTS 45 (1944) 151-157.

Roche, Michael de. "Yahweh's Rîb Against Israel: A Re-Assessment of the So-Called 'Prophetic Lawsuit' in the Pre-exilic Prophets," JBL 102 (1983) 563-574.

Rofé, Alexander. The Book of Balaam (Hebrew). Jerusalem: Simor, 1979.

Roskoff, Gustav. *Geschichte des Teufels*. Leipzig: Brockhaus, 1869.

Ross, James F. "Job 33:14-30: The Phenomenology of Lament," *JBL* 94 (1975) 38-46.

Rothstein, J. W. *Die Nachtgesichte des Sacharja*. Leipzig: Hinrichs, 1910.

__________, and Hänel, D. J. *Kommentar zum ersten Buch der Chronik*. KAT 18; Leipzig: Scholl, 1927.

Rouillard, H. "L'ânesse de Balaam," *RB* 87 (1980) 5-37, 211-239.

Rowley, H. H. *Job*. CB; Don Mills: Thomas Nelson and Sons, 1970.

Rudolph, Wilhelm. *Der "Elohist" von Exodus bis Joshua*. Berlin: Alfred Töpelmann, 1938.

__________. *Haggai-Sacharja 1-8- Sacharja 9-14- Maleachi*. KAT 13; Gütersloh: Gerd Mohn, 1976.

Rupprecht, Konrad. "Die Zuverlässigkeit der Uberlieferung von Salomos Tempelgrundung," *ZAW* 89 (1977) 205-214.

Rüthy, A. E. "Seben Augen auf einem Stein," *TZ* 13 (1957) 523-529.

Ryder, Stuart A. *The D-Stem in Western Semitic*. Paris: Mouton, 1974.

Sarna, Nahum M. "Epic Substratum in the Book of Job," *JBL* 76 (1957) 13-25.

Schlatter, Adolf. *Der Evangelist Matthaüs*. Stuttgart: Calwer, 1957.

Schmid, H. "Der Tempelbau Solomos in religionsgeschichtlicher Sicht," A. Kuschke (ed.), *Archäologie und Altes Testament*, 241-250. Tübingen: J.C.B. Mohr, 1970.

Schmid, H. H. "Creation, Righteousness, and Salvation," B. W. Anderson (ed.), *Creation in the Old Testament*, 102-117. Philadelphia: Fortress, 1984.

__________. *Die sogenannten Jahwist*. Zurich: Theologischer, 1976.

Schmidt, Hans. *Die Psalmen*. HAT; Tübingen: J.C.B. Mohr,

1934.

__________. "Das vierte Nachtgesicht des Propheten Sacharja," ZAW 54 (1936) 48-60.

Schmidt, Ludwig. "Die alttestamentliche Bileamüberlieferung," BZ 23 (1979) 234-261.

Scholnick, Sylvia H. "The Meaning of mišpāṭ in the Book of Job," JBL 101 (1982) 521-529.

Schottroff, Willy. "Zur Sozialgeschichte Israels in der Perserzeit," Verkündigung und Forschung 27 (1982) 46-68.

Seeligmann, I. L. "Zur Terminologie für das Gerichtsverfahren in Wortschatz biblischen Hebräisch," VTSup 16 (1967) 251-278.

Seybold, Klaus. Bilder zum Tempelbau. Stuttgart: K. B. W., 1974.

Simon, Uriel. "The Poor Man's Ewe-Lamb: An Example of a Juridical Parable," Biblica 48 (1967) 207-242.

Speer, Julius. "Zur Exegese von Hiob 19,25-27," ZAW 25 (1905) 47-140.

Speiser, E. A. "Census and Ritual Expiation in Mari and Israel," BASOR 149 (1958) 17-25.

Stade, B. Geschichte des Volkes Israel. Berlin: G. Grote, 1888.

Stinespring, W. F. "Eschatology in Chronicles," JBL 80 (1961) 209-219.

Strack, H. L. and Billerbeck, P. Kommentar zum Neuen Testament aus Talmud und Midrasch. Munich: C. H. Beck, 1956.

Taylor, Vincent. The Gospel According to Mark. London: MacMillan, 1966.

Terrien, Samuel. Job: Poet of Existence. New York: Bobbs Merrill, 1957.

Thomas, D. Winton. "A Note on mḥlṣwt in Zechariah 3:4," JTS 33 (1932) 279-280.

__________. "Zechariah," IB vol. 6, 1053-1114.

Throntveit, Mark A. "Linguistic Analysis and the Question of Authorship in Chronicles, Ezra, Nehemia," VT 32 (1982)

201-216.

Thureau-Dangin, F. Rituels akkadiens. Osnabrück: Otto Zeller, 1975.

Tidwell, N. "Wāʾōmar (Zech 3:5) and the Genre of Zechariah's Fourth Vision," JBL 94 (1975) 343-355.

Trachtenberg, Joshua. The Devil and the Jews: The Medieval Conception of the Jew and Its Relation to Modern Anti-Semitism. New Haven: Yale University, 1943; republished, Philadelphia: Jewish Publication Society, 1983.

Tsevat, Matitiahu. The Meaning of the Book of Job and Other Bible Studies. New York: Ktav, 1980.

Tur-Sinai, N. H. The Book of Job. Jerusalem: Kiryath Sepher, 1957.

__________. "How Satan Came into the World," Expository Times, 1936/7.

Ulrich, Eugene Charles. The Qumran Text of Samuel and Josephus. HSM 19; Missoula: Scholars, 1978.

Urbrock, William J. "Oral Antecedents to Job: A Survey of Formulas and Formulaic Systems," Semeia 5 (1976) 111-137.

Vaulx, J. de. Les Nombres. Paris: Gabalda, 1972.

Vaux, Roland de. Ancient Israel: Its Life and Institutions. New York: McGraw-Hill, 1961.

__________. "Titres et functionnaires égyptiens à la cour de David et de Salomon," RB 48 (1939) 394-405.

Vermes, Geza. Scripture and Tradition in Judaism: Haggadic Studies. Leiden: Brill, 1973.

Vorlander, Hermann. Mein Gott: Die Vorstellungen vom persönliche Gott im Alten Orient und Alten Testament. AOAT 23; Neukirchen-Vluyn: Neukirchener, 1975.

Weippert, Helga und Manfred. "Die 'Bileam' Inschrift von Tell Deir ʿAllā," ZDPV 98 (1982) 77-103.

Weiser, Artur. The Psalms. OTL; Philadelphia: SCM, 1962.

Weiss, Meir. The Story of Job's Beginning: Job 1-2: A Literary Analysis. Jerusalem: Magnes, 1983.

Whedbee, William. "The Comedy of Job," Semeia 7 (1977) 1-39.

Williams, James G. "'You Have Not Spoken Truth of Me:' Mystery and Irony in Job," ZAW 83 (1971) 231-255.

Williams, Ronald J. "Current Trends in the Study of the Book of Job," Walter E. Aufrecht (ed.), Studies in the Book of Job, 1-27. Waterloo: Wilfred Laurier, 1985.

Williamson, H. G. M. 1 and 2 Chronicles. Grand Rapids: Eerdmans, 1982.

__________. Israel in the Book of Chronicles. Cambridge: Cambridge University, 1977.

Wright, G. Ernest. See Boling.

__________. "The Lawsuit of God: A Form-Critical Study of Deuteronomy 32," B. W. Anderson and W. Harrelson (eds.), Israel's Prophetic Heritage. New York: Harper, 1962.

__________. The Old Testament Against its Enviroment. Chicago: Henry Regnery, 1950.

Yadin, Yigael. The Scroll of the War of the Sons of Light Against the Sons of Darkness. Oxford: Oxford University, 1962.

Zannoni, Arthur E. "Balaam: International Seer/Wizard Prophet," St. Luke's Journal of Theology 22 (1978) 5-19.

Zimmermann, F. "Folk Etymology of Biblical Names," VTSup 15 (1965) 311-326.

Zimmern, Henrico. Akkadische Fremdwörter als Beweis für babylonischen Kultureinfluss. Leipzig: Hinrichs, 1914.

__________. Die Keilinschriften und das Alten Testament, vol. 2. Berlin: Reuther, 1902.

Zink, James K. "Impatient Job: An Interpretation of Job 19:25-27," JBL 84 (1965) 147-152.